THE
LEFTOVERS
OF
WAR

ROGER FARROW

The majority of the images in this book
are from the author's collection.

Every attempt has been made to gain permission for the use of
images not from the author's collection in this book.
Any omissions will be rectified in future editions.

The moral right of the author has been asserted.

A full CIP record for this book is available from the British Library.

First published in 2023 by
Riverside Publishing Solutions, Salisbury, UK

www.riversidepublishingsolutions.com

Printed and bound in the UK.

Dedication

To Bob Nesbitt, Spike Kelly, Billy Neil, George Cooney, Gordon Whipp, Bernie Roome, Dave Kinnon, Phil Monks, Ron Tobin, Maurice Winter, Jim Gore; Bomb Disposal and attached, my comrades who are no longer with us.

And to Les Wardle, who suffered most but received no recognition.

Contents

Foreword

This is not a novel, nor is it a history of Bomb Disposal, a subject already in print, written by those far better placed and more qualified than I. However, for the purposes of background information, certain facts need to be extracted, as one can't assume every reader will be conversant with what is after all, an obscure line of work. The majority historical record has been produced by officers and this book, therefore, is my attempt to show the job from a ranker's point of view. As such, I will submit a personal collection of thumbnail portraits, anecdotes, true stories, and photographs, of everyday life and various tasks undertaken by real people, ordinary soldiers of a bomb disposal unit within which I served so many years ago. It was once described as being trapped in a time warp. It could not have taken place elsewhere and would certainly not happen today! Many things I might well have forgotten, but many memories are still fresh, made so by the incomparable comradeship we had then and, in some cases, still have.

Bomb Disposal, as it was then known, still makes headlines occasionally, although with the advent of time, there are fewer incidents. Most of the bombs have now been found and disposed of; there are some still left in the Thames and other main rivers, and they are at some depth.

The following pages will recount several incidents that I recall during my service with the unit. It's fair to say that these incidents, both at work and play, formed the most intense and interesting part of my working life. For two and a half years, I had experiences unequalled by anything, before or since.

Acknowledgements

My thanks to Dave Stone, for his newspaper articles and his military history, to John Green, for his newspaper photo of the Hammersmith bomb job and to Brian 'Scouse' Manning and Dave Woolmer for their reminiscences. Most thanks go to Stuart Ingrey, for all his stories, reminders, and corrections, without whom this book would never have seen the light of day. Much detail has been drawn from 'Unexploded Bomb' by the late Maj. A.B. Hartley MBE RE Cassel 1958. Last but most importantly, my thanks to my wife Lai, who has had to put up with me.

The Exodus

It was a typical cold, overcast, English day in February 1967 when we left Chattenden Barracks. Wednesday the 22nd to be precise. We'd had a going-away session in the NAAFI the previous evening and most of the single blokes were feeling a bit fragile. Bob Nesbitt and I had made a beeline to a table occupied by several WRAC girls, only to be told by a pretty redhead that they don't like men! There were many like them in the WRAC in those days. What a waste! So, with us having been put in our place, Bob and I teamed up with others in the section due to leave the next day. We made a big event out of our departure and got thoroughly plastered. We declined the request to leave the NAAFI at "last orders" and the guard was called out; we left!

Thirteen blokes looking the worst for wear at the side of the barrack square, waiting for transport, was evidence enough that the previous night had been a good one.

As luck would have it, a good friend of mine happened to be working on the barrack square at the time, working on sapper toys. His Troop Sergeant gave him five minutes to see us off. We said our goodbyes and he and I promised we would stay in touch; and we did. He had applied to go on the job with us but was not accepted. Instead, he was posted out. Bomb Disposal's loss and 50 Squadron's gain.

By this time our transport had arrived, and we loaded our luggage and gingerly climbed aboard. The trip to Heathrow was much the same as any trip in a 3-ton Bedford. If you sat too near the tailboard, you were almost asphyxiated by exhaust fumes but if you sat further in, you saw nothing. I spent a lot of that trip just dozing and I suspect I wasn't the only one.

On arrival at Heathrow, we went into the concourse and looked around. This would be my first trip anywhere and it was all new to me. A couple of the lads had served in BAOR, and one had seen service in the Radfan, so had travelled before but most of us were first timers. My brother had journeyed to Heathrow to see me off, but it was a brief farewell as our sergeant, George Duncan, was anxious to be going into departures. Maybe he was worried we'd all have gone AWOL if we weren't trapped behind the departure barrier. We were his responsibility after all. The OC had left for Singapore on the 7th February so he was in the Far East already. I bought myself 50 Senior Service Cigarettes at Duty Free and opened the box, only to be pounced on by a Customs officer, who promptly resealed the box and told me I could only open them when airborne. We all have to learn.

We boarded our flight, a British Eagle Viscount, the normal armed forces mode of air travel at that time. We were still in the era of turbo props and this trip, with stops, took us 26 hours! There was plenty of beer for all on board and contrary to normal behaviour now, no one was sick, no one got into a fight and the women and kids comprising the families of serving personnel were safe and well looked after.

Our first stop was in Frankfurt, where we all stayed on board. Our next real break was in Kuwait, where there was a leg stretch for two hours, time to wander around the concourse.

It was nighttime, I recall. I poked my head out of a doorway and was confronted by a Kuwaiti soldier with an SMG, who pointed it at me and indicated that I get back inside. Happy to mate, keep your finger off the trigger! Kuwait is best remembered for that and the smell of stale coffee and old cigars. It might have been more memorable if it wasn't for the fact that it was in the early hours of the morning, and I was tired. After hours more travel, much of it spent drinking beer, with which the flight was apparently well stocked, we arrived at Colombo, Ceylon, long before it was renamed Sri Lanka.

I was glad to get off the plane and stretch my legs. I'd been seated with a bloke I barely knew. His name was Phillips. I never knew his first name, but he was Welsh, so he was 'Taff'. For many of us on board, soldiers, and families, this was our first flight, and some show of travel nerves were in evidence, but the sun was shining, all was right with the world, and we had some time to kill before resuming our trip. So, we ordered beers, sat at tables at the side of the runway and relaxed in the sun. I'd been drinking cans of light ale on the plane, but I drank lager in Ceylon. I'd never tasted this before. In England I drank light-and-bitter, mild-and-bitter, stout-and-bitter, brown-and-mild, or just plain bitter and I wasn't impressed with this new drink.

Some of the lads had a photo taken with the air hostesses and then we got under way again, heading for our destination, Singapore, where we landed at midnight (eight hours in advance of UK time). It was good to get off and walk about. No complaints about British Eagle's service, food, or anything else and I've had worse since then and paid a lot for it.

The first impression I had of Singapore was the heat and the smell. My shirt stuck to me as I got off the aircraft and the smell hit us in a palpable wave, and I asked myself what sort of place had we come to. Payar Lebur, which was the international airport back then, was next to the municipal rubbish tip. But we'd arrived and for the reasons behind our arrival, we have to turn back the clock.

Left to Right; Park, Gordon Whipp, Bob Nesbitt, Mick Rose, John Green
Colombo, February 1967

PART ONE

Chapter One

Where It All Began

I presented myself at the Guardroom of the Royal Engineers Bomb Disposal unit at Broadbridge Heath, Sussex on 2nd January 1966. I came straight from Training Regiment and was more than a little apprehensive, (although this apprehension was as nothing compared to finding myself outside the main gate of No 1 Training Regiment five months previously). It's a peculiarity of my memory that I can remember nothing more of my arrival; not who I reported to in the guardroom or who took me to the billet. While in training I'd been part of a group. Now, I was on my own, or so I thought. I needn't have worried. There were two more blokes I knew from the same training party posted there, both of whom arrived on the same day.

I was allocated a bed space and kitted out. Then it was up to me. We were billeted in spiders, as we had been in training, so the accommodation was familiar. But everything else was new and it was with some trepidation that I awaited what tomorrow might bring. The first couple of hours were taken up with sorting out the bedspace and putting my kit away in a locker. I found the lads in the room were friendly enough to the new boys.

All three of us were billeted in the same room, as part of 2 Troop, 49 Bomb Disposal Squadron.

In the same room, in no particular order, were Lance Corporals Dave Stone, Ian McGeachin, Sid Davis and Andy McAndrew. The sapper contingent was made up of Cochran, Vismer, Eden, Winton, Roome, Gore, Gillon, Wardle and myself.

Unusual for a military establishment, there was also a civvy billeted in the room, a big 'Geordie' named Hutton. He drove a section 3-ton truck. A Sapper Ingrey was still due to arrive.

First-parade the next morning came as a shock. I saw more different types of uniform at one time than I thought possible. There were No2 dress, civvies and denims, but denims with variations; denims with waders, denims with wellies, denims with DMS boots, even woolly pullovers and leather jerkins of the type favoured by sappers of the last war. The headgear was equally varied; berets, No1 dress hats and miners' helmets. Mostly miners' helmets, in fact. The parade was taken by a corporal, 'Sam' Sissons. He was called Sam because that's how he addressed everyone else. The SSM, 'Jersey' Morshead very rarely left his office at the top end of the square to show up on first parade. That area housed the offices of the CO, RSM and Squadron Administration offices. Our Chief Clerk, WO2 Smitherman, known to the troops as Mary, also had his office there. He was a nice old boy, coming up for his discharge and had medals from way back, as had several soldiers in that unit. As the roll was called, one voice came from inside the billet.

This was a real eye-opener but the excuse for this lack of discipline was that we were a working unit, with crews spread around the country and the job came first. Not a lot of time was devoted to bull in the ordinary week.

A familiar sight in the camp were two Royal Observer Corps personnel, a middle-aged man, and a woman. They had an office and had in it a telephone, binoculars and many wall charts depicting German aircraft circa 1940.

They wore RAF style blue battledress, also of 1940's vintage. They had been operational since 1925 and contributed much to the defence of our land throughout WW2 and later, during the Cold War but 'Options for Change' instituted by penny-pinching politicians, who had no sense of loyalty, saw their demise. 10,500 ROC personnel were stood down in 1995.

Apart from it being my new home, this camp housed the Joint Services Bomb Disposal School and there was a bomb museum, chock full of exhibits, from the smallest piece of mischief to really huge munitions. The larger ones were arrayed in rows outside the school and were always the first thing to catch the eye, some being painted in bright colours. We were told to keep away from this part of the camp for a while. Despite its appearance the JSBDS was world renowned and military personnel came from many nations to be taught the methods of bomb disposal. If my memory serves me correctly, the chief instructor of the school at that time was a Royal Navy officer, a Lieut. Commander Honour, but it was a rotational appointment.

Bomb alley at the JSBDS

Stuart Ingrey recalled that when he eventually arrived, the first thing he can remember was the door of the billet being opened and seeing an arrow fly the length of the billet and bury itself in the further door. This was fired by one Sapper Frank Baker. Frank was intellectually quite bright but had the commonsense of an empty bottle, as the arrow episode proved and this wasn't the only time he performed this nonsensical act. But, as he was known to do stupid things, no one said anything about him using a bow in the building. Stuart's next shock was the morning parade. Having just come from BAOR, this was a real experience, but he was personally going to contribute to this eccentric array in the near future, wearing waders and a duffel coat on many a first parade. This mode of dress is what he travelled in, to and from his home near Chichester. With little time to change into a different uniform, he cut his losses and came prepared.

Three days after my arrival, there was a death in the unit. One of the corporals out on detachment on mine clearance, Corporal J Farthing, had died, presumably of natural causes. I'm told there was a firing party, and the man was buried with full military honours. This seemed like a bad omen to me.

About a week after arrival, I went with a section to Dungeness in Kent. The task was to sweep the beach for mines, using 4C Mine Detectors. Travelling down to Kent in the back of a 3-ton truck was a trial. We were freezing, even though dressed in cold weather kit. In good weather it would have been enjoyable, but this was January, and it was Arctic. Arriving at Dungeness, we were greeted by a bleak and forbidding landscape. All around were metal portacabins, which apart from being used as stores, we were also expected to sleep in.

The place was full of Irish labourers, employed by McAlpine, the building contractor. The labourers had a canteen and there were generally several hundred of them in there knocking back Guinness, which was all that was on sale. They sang Irish rebel songs and acted like fools, but they had no trouble with us. It was a chaotic scene outside, with machinery everywhere.

There was knee-deep snow on the ground and in these conditions, we had to attempt to sweep the pebble beach, and Dungeness has one of the largest areas of pebbles in Europe. On one sweep, Stu Ingrey was working in one lane as shovel man and Sailor Roome, in another lane using the 4C. Sailor was making wide arcs and continually tapping Stuart's heels with the machine. It got so bad that Stu snapped, turned round, and hit Sailor in the middle with his shovel, which caught Sailor on his belt buckle and knocked him down. It stopped him messing around.

There was no harm in trying to make a bad job more enjoyable, but no one needed extra aggravation on a dangerous task like that. All was well later and no hard feelings. The weather conditions meant that this was not the best introduction to our new job but in another, it showed us immediately what might be expected of us in the future. As far as anyone can remember, if there were heaters in the portacabins we lived in, they were not efficient. I was sharing one with Stuart Ingrey.

We froze inside these metal boxes and at nighttime we slept in duffle coats. Conditions were that bad! As luck would have it, our section was recalled after a few days, to go on another job, leaving others to carry on the work. Stuart said the snow was so deep one morning that they couldn't find the D7 armoured bulldozer. It was eventually located and 'Cat' Preston, the plant operator, started it up and blew a huge jet of snow in the air. Said one of McAlpine's finest, 'They've brought a fockin' tank!' It was so cold, the mine detector batteries almost failed but as they had long leads, they were taken out of the detectors and put in the pocket and this solved the problem.

With white lane marking tapes on top of the snow, it was difficult to see them, and the depth of snow interfered with the machine's function. One day work stopped and for amusement, the lads threw themselves out of the back of a moving 3-ton truck, travelling at 20mph. It must have been something to do with hearing about the Parachute Regiment. This was one of the Para tests, but they did it at 30mph. That job lasted some weeks and was classed as difficult.

Some jobs were even more so. While we laboured there, others of the unit, with Royal Navy personnel, were engaged in the lifting of a 250kg bomb from the river Thames. Divers had been checking the abutments of Blackfriars Bridge and they found the bomb embedded in the concrete. This was eventually hauled out, removed to a safe place, and detonated.

After leaving Dungeness, we returned to Broadbridge Heath, where I was reassigned to a different section and we went off to the wilds of the Midlands. We were working on a farm in Hollywood, Birmingham and we were in a hole, literally and figuratively. The hole in question had appeared next to a footpath which ran through the farm and members of the public had approached the farmer and asked him to do something about it because someone might fall in. I have no idea whether there had been any bombing in that area during the war years, but something must have triggered this investigation.

Our section was led by a sergeant, Frank F, a dour Scot. He was aided and abetted by a great character; an old soldier named George Cooney. George was a lance corporal and sported a waxed moustache and wore WW2 and Korea ribbons on his tunic. What official function George had in that section, I never knew but he was there. I fell afoul of our sergeant early on. He pulled me up one day and told me to put my beret on properly. I had it too far over the front of my head. He asked me if I thought I was some sort of a tough guy, to which I answered 'no'. He then told me to wear my beret in the proper manner from then on. What wearing a hat had to do with being tough

I couldn't say. And on another occasion, after I'd called him sarge, he said to me that he didn't call me sap so I should address him as sergeant, not sarge. All technically correct but pretty narrow-minded. I was to discover this was always his attitude with us.

Our equipment was carried to the site on a 3-ton truck and getting the vehicle across those muddy fields was difficult. At one stage, the truck broke through a bridge over a stream and the culvert had to be repaired. On that job, if something could go wrong, it did!

We spent 6 weeks digging in that hole and we froze. I had an awful cold, which turned to flu. I was off the job for a few days, recuperating in the infantry barracks at Sutton Coldfield, then back to work. Morning after morning we rose to grey skies and bad weather conditions, had breakfast, and went to the field where we dug, cursed and floundered in the mud.

Every day, a tent was erected on site but only George Cooney and our sergeant used it, Cooney to make tea and Sgt F for shelter. Like many of the jobs we were to encounter, it was soul destroying work and as fast as we dug, the soil fell back in twice as fast and digging down, in hail, rain and snow, we broke through land drains, which flooded the hole, which then had to be pumped out. We worked sometimes up to our knees in mud and filth.

Due to all the water, one day the sides of the hole completely collapsed, and we had to wait for the arrival of a Calweld excavator, operated by one Lance corporal Lou Sheldrake, known to us as Shellshock.

This machine dug a round hole about eight feet in diameter in super-fast time and curved, fibre-glass sections were then bolted in place, keeping the soil from falling back. The soil didn't fall in but I did. A plank was run across the hole and Sapper 'Harry' Wragg, our plant operator, and me were standing on the plank, using an auger. We braced ourselves prior to pulling the auger out and while straightening our legs, the plank snapped in half and deposited us both at the bottom of the hole. The soil was soft almost to the point of liquidity, so neither of us were injured. Filthy, yes, but unharmed. It was like paddling about in treacle!

We lived in digs, as sections often did while out working. Ours were in the Adelphi Café at Hay Mills, Birmingham. There, four of us shared a room and were given a very substantial breakfast and evening meal. The café was owned by a family named Clifford. They had a daughter, Wendy. Mum and dad Clifford asked me if I'd mind taking their daughter to the pictures. She wanted to see a Doris Day, Rock Hudson film but couldn't go on her own and her parents were too busy to take her. It was the last film I wanted to see but it wouldn't hurt, so I escorted her. It was nice to be trusted. I was entertained later at her home by her parents. They were a nice family.

Apart from the end of job drink, I can think of no time when we went out drinking at local pubs, being quite content to stay in the café during the evening, listening to the jukebox and drinking coffee. For one thing, being winter, the weather wasn't exactly made for traipsing the streets, pub hunting.

One of the joys of being in this unit was the fact that we drew subsistence pay. If there was a military establishment nearby, either regular or TA, we would have to live there and be paid regular army wages but there was seldom such an establishment and so we had to rely on civilian accommodation. In 1966, we were drawing about seventeen pounds sterling per person, per week, while away from camp. Being on a six-year engagement, my normal pay was six pounds per week so seventeen was very good money to me. This was obviously paid to enable us to live in B&B's. Needless to say, there was every effort to see that the cash was spent on beer. Some slept in the Bedford truck and two slept in a tent to my knowledge.

The end result of that six week's work was a three-foot iron bar. How it found its way fifteen feet underground remains one of life's mysteries. The bomb locator had traced a metal object and we had to find out what it was. Said the farmer's wife, 'I never thought there was a bomb there anyway. I never lost any sleep over it'.

When this job was wrapped up, we had a decent party in a Birmingham pub and it was during this event that a very drunk 'Scouse' Gore confronted Sgt F and called him a short-arsed, bandy-legged, ginger-haired, piggy-eyed, broken-nosed little Jock bastard.

We stood by, waiting to see what would happen but there was no response at all. I'm sure that Sgt F knew as we all did that Scouse was just a bag of wind. Nothing was even said the next day when Scouse was sober.

Our sergeant was all the things that Scouse said and a thoroughly unlikeable person but to my mind, he was also a hard little sod and would have chewed Scouse to bits and spat his shirt buttons out.

Scouse was instrumental in introducing me to some wonderful people, his family. He asked me to hitchhike with him to Liverpool one weekend while on the Birmingham job and having never hitched anywhere before, I thought I'd give it a try. We duly set out on a Saturday morning and soon got a lift in a truck that took us about halfway. It was easy back then to pick up a lift and with another quick trip on a truck, we were dropped off at Kirkby, outside a well-known watering hole called the Cherry Tree. After a couple of pints, we made our way to his home, where I was made a great fuss of. Scouse's mum, on finding that my own mum had died when I was young, made me an adopted son. I went back there on other trips and received the same reception.

Birmingham
Sissons & Farrow checking the morass we left behind

Mrs. Gore even made a separate trifle for me on Sunday afternoons when we went back there. She also adopted big Tim Vismer, him being so far from home. Grand people!

The opportunity to live as normal human beings was a great help while on this job. We were continually being treated like children by our sergeant, so being accepted by the Gores and being spoilt was wonderful.

The Hollywood task being completed, the crew were sent to Lutterworth, near Rugby and we left behind at Warren Farm in Birmingham, a wasteland of mud that had to be cordoned off with barbed wire and pickets.

The Lutterworth site

The Lutterworth job was also in a field, a sea of mud between two rivers and the shaft had to be continuously pumped out.

It was yet another foul, wet, thoroughly miserable job, one that tested the resources and capability of the team involved

The shaft
Tim Vismer standing and Stu Ingrey leaving the shaft

to the utmost and one which they resolutely stuck to and completed; a good team, Kinnon, Ingrey, Vismer, Green, Wardle, McAndrew, d'Arcy, Eden, Davis and Potter. More came as they were freed from other tasks. A bomb had indeed been dropped here and Stu Ingrey remembered finding a tail fin measuring about two and half feet long at a depth of 12 feet. There was ample evidence of shrapnel, indicating that the bomb, a large one, had exploded underground without leaving a camouflet, probably due to the wet conditions.

While on this task, I came into contact with some strange beings. Our accommodation was in what came to be known as the Tramp's Hostel, aka The Poor Farm. Most of the inmates were down-and-outs, derelicts with nowhere else to go. Some were obviously well on the way to senility, poor souls. However, when you have a hard day's digging in front of you, the last thing you need is some loony knocking on the door at 01:00.

I shared a room with Stu Ingrey and it was here that we found nocturnal sounds and loud voices were a regular occurrence. The first time this happened, I was just drifting off to sleep. I shouted at this nuisance and asked what he wanted but there was no reply. Then more knocking. Stu told him to take himself off and I was much more explicit, but it happened on more occasions.

This was also the place where I had little to eat and I don't know how I survived. We usually ate breakfast at the local 'greasy spoon', the name for a transport café, where a big fry-up was consumed prior to starting the day's work. Very unhealthy by today's standards but we needed the intake to see us through the following hours of work. This was necessary because the food served up for our evening meal was grim, unnamed pieces of fat and gristle floating about in watery gruel; basic, badly cooked food. Even the potatoes were liquid. Sitting at long tables, in a high-ceilinged dining hall, straight out of a Dickensian workhouse, Stuart ate his own meals and mine too. I told him I couldn't stomach this muck and he said if I didn't mind, he'd eat mine too, which he did. He was a big boy, about six feet tall and needed it. If the condition of the food hadn't put me off my appetite, the sight of dribbling old men, snuffling over their rations would have. As a fairly fit twenty-one-year-old, my wish was for God to preserve me from ending up like that!

Had it not been for the local pub, the Lord Raglan, where during the evening I had a ham sandwich with my pint, I'd have wasted away. Luckily, (or unluckily, depending on how you look at it) I was served up with swill like this only once more in my life and that was in the cookhouse of the Grenadier Guards, in the Caribbean.

Stu and I forged a friendship in the Poor Farm that's lasted until today, when we're both on the wrong side of 70! Many times we shared the last smoke and a pint. Thrift wasn't part of our vocabulary, and we quite often ran short of cash.

It was in the pub each evening that Stuart and I talked about our previous life experiences and our aspirations for the future. We discussed wildlife and found that we both had the same interest. Other topics came and went and made the evenings enjoyable. We were chalk and cheese really, but we hit it off well. My background must have seemed very different to anything he'd known while his was equally strange to me.

They say that opposites attract, and, in our case, they did! I was a big city boy and he was a country boy, what we used to call a swede. The greatest draw we had was an abiding interest in all things Viking. Mine had been awakened by reading the life of Olaf Tryggvison, Olaf the Glorious, King of Norway. What prompted Stu's interest I have no idea. It was enough that he had one! Our evenings were spent just talking, no jukeboxes or piped music, just chat.

Stuart was an enigma to me. He was well spoken and seemed educated. He was two years younger than I but had been in the army longer.

Both his grandfather and father had been army officers, so what was this man doing as a sapper? It turned out that Stu had enlisted as POM, (potential officer material) and had duly been sent on an officer training course. However, I was told that one night round a campfire, when during a discussion he was asked what his opinion was, he told them that he thought they were all talking a load of shit! It wasn't appreciated and back went Stu to his unit and was a sapper from then on.

STUART INGREY

Stuart joined the army in July 1964 and went to Training Regiment, Royal Engineers. He originally wanted to join his county regiment, the Royal Sussex Regiment, but his father wouldn't agree to this. He wasn't to join the PBI the (poor bloody infantry).

Stuart's father had boyhood memories of his father going off to the Great War and its awful waste of life. He had nothing against the Royal Engineers but wouldn't let his son join Boy Service. Stu could have completed his education had he been allowed to join as a boy entrant. However, he had to wait until he'd passed his seventeenth birthday before he could join man's service and even then, his father insisted he joined as a OR1, which meant that he attended a WOSB for promotion to officer. He spent two or three days at Westbury in Wiltshire, doing command tasks and initiative tests.

The applicants had to get across an imaginary ravine with the aid of poles, planks, cordage and oil drums etc. then negotiate obstacles using the same equipment. They took it in turns to be in charge and to lecture. All the time they were under close observation by officers with millboards. Even during mealtimes, they were monitored, presumably to see whether they could use a knife and fork correctly. Stuart was unaware of the end result.

Later, he was sent for some weeks to Beaconsfield in Buckinghamshire for preliminary education to improve his ACE (Army Certificate of Education) class three results. He'd never passed a mathematics exam in his life so thought this was all a waste of time.

His first posting was to the School of Military Survey at Hermitage, near Newbury and was in 86 Survey Training Squadron. He was supposed to do aptitude tests but in his opinion, there was no hurry and he settled down to do very little and he ended up with the job of assistant bedding storeman. There was an old civilian who, in Stuart's words, was quite capable of doing the job and didn't need any help as bedding issues only took place when personnel were posted in or out. Occasionally Stuart threw some mothballs around or counted blankets and he lit the pot-bellied stove and read books. This routine was broken only by shovelling snow from the doors and tracks. It was a cushy life, interrupted by NAAFI breaks and mealtimes but he found first parade troublesome and was determined to find a way out of attending that.

NCOs studying 'A' trade surveyor courses needed help to 'shoot' the stars, so he volunteered his services.

On bright, frosty nights, a table would be set up on the square and the NCO would take his sightings. Stuart filled in the azimuth readings and operated the stopwatch. When this was completed, they'd repair to a hut where the NCO would compute his findings and Stu would make tea. If he worked until midnight, he'd be excused first parade, but if he worked after midnight, he was given the whole morning off. This went on for some time but eventually someone got wise to this and he and about eight others were posted to Germany.

Stuart was put in charge of the group and en-route, they stopped off in London for one night, sleeping at the Union Jack Club, near Waterloo Station. Next morning one man was missing but he turned up before they left for Gatwick Airport. Gatwick was then a one-story building and passengers had to walk out on to the tarmac to board the aircraft. They were given a bollocking for smoking while walking out to the aircraft.

They were all posted as general duties men to 14 Field Survey Squadron, based at Ratingen, near Dusseldorf and they did all sorts of jobs; guarding ammunition trains was a favourite. Stuart also worked in the MT, and in the QM's, where he was given the task of disposing of security waste. As this was before shredders, he had to burn everything and he did so, sheet by sheet, thereby taking his time.

Germany meant military exercises and while the squadrons chased around the East German Plain, he and his gang did all the camp jobs and provided picquets and patrols. They went foraging and looting and had some

Stu Ingrey
Chattenden 1966

memorable adventures. They worked in the cookhouse, mainly washing dishes and they dug refuse pits and latrines.

Stuart was standing guard one night in the security block and found an unlocked office door. He browsed through files and found information regarding stevedores which he thought looked interesting but that would mean leaving the Corps for the RCT; he didn't want that. He also found material about Bomb Disposal and thought he might have a crack at that. His father had served in this discipline during the war. His application was initially turned down, but he persevered and was finally accepted. As snow began to fall on Westphalia, he was on his way home, where he spent Christmas. He reported back to Survey School one day late, was charged and fined one week's stoppage of pay and he reported to HQ Bomb Disposal on 4th January 1966, thereby starting our life-long friendship.

Along with Sapper Phil Monks, Mick Scott driving, I returned to Broadbridge Heath in March, coming back by way of a fairly large town, the name of which I never knew. We were halted by a big traffic jam. This promised to keep us on the road for ages, so Mick switched on the blue light and the bell. Vehicles then made way for us. We sped through, bell ringing and congratulating Mick on his quick thinking. But we were brought down to earth when we got back to camp. Someone in the civil authority had been informed about this and a report was sent to HQ; unauthorised use of bell and blue light, don't let it happen again. It never affected Phil or me, we were just passengers but Mick copped it. Phil had been on the Lutterworth dig and was the owner of a battered old, hand-painted green van. He drove us around the towns in that area during weekends and, being a local boy there, had, on a Sunday evening, introduced us to Derby, the pearl of the Midlands.

Derby on a Sunday evening was a non-place! He also took us to other exotic locations. I can't recall seeing a less interesting place to live. I assumed he left his passion wagon with family because he never took it back to Sussex.

Chapter Two

We came back to a proper lifestyle and back to huge meals prepared by Big Louie, our civilian cook. After Lutterworth I needed some real food and there we awaited the next job. It was a strange fact that civilians made up a larger proportion of the workforce than military personnel. According to sources, there were 80 soldiers and about 200 civilians in the unit. There was a gang of Ukrainians permanently working in Hampshire and another at Storrington.

These Ukrainians were ex-prisoners of war, who'd fought in German uniform. Unlike their compatriots, they weren't sent back to the tender mercies of Joe Stalin under the Yalta Agreements but were put to work digging up bombs. A far better prospect than the inevitable death sentence of repatriation. A lot of Ukrainians had been inducted into the SS, as were many others of the occupied countries and every one of those who worked alongside us had been members of the 14th Galizian SS Division. They were part of the more than eight thousand seven hundred ex-Ukrainian SS men allowed to live in Britain by a government that was perfectly willing to use them for spying and other clandestine jobs but admit nothing to the British public. Subsequent governments have kept a lid on this but more and more information is now coming to light.

All those who had a hand in this disgraceful state of affairs are now dead, so can't be made to answer for their actions but the public have a right to know why these enemy soldiers were allowed to live in Britain. It was understood by the German High Command that these men would never be ordered to fight western troops, only Russians, which is what they did, so they weren't classed as enemy aliens by the British government. This Ukrainian division was responsible for a long list of war crimes in Eastern Europe, war crimes they should have been made to answer for but as the said crimes weren't committed against the west, they got away Scot-free.

Small price to pay not seeing your homeland again if the alternative was a Joe Stalin firing squad. The Russians, of course, could not crow about this as they had their very own SS division, in the shape of the 30th.

Other occupied countries had their own SS divisions, Latvia had the 15th and 19th, Estonia the 20th, Hungary the 25th and 26th, Belgium the 27th and 28th, Italy the 29th, France the 33rd and Holland, the 23rd and 34th. None of these countries can point the finger at another regarding collaboration as they were all equally guilty. All had thousands of young men more than willing to serve in this, the most hated and evil organisation on earth.

There were a lot of ex-displaced persons on camp, left-overs from the last war. Stu Ingrey recalls; 'Coke Smoke' was a Greek and operated the boilers. He gave his pay to Horsham hospital among other recipients. There was 'Fat Willie', a German, reputed to be ex-SS and looked the part. Willie slept in a chair, never in a bed. Maybe that was due to his bulk. Adolf, in charge of the timber store was so named because of his resemblance to Hitler, complete with toothbrush moustache and funny haircut. Helmut, another German said that we were lucky that Hitler was mad, otherwise they (Germany) would have won the war.

Little Charlie must have a mention. He pottered about the camp, pulling a four-wheeled cart on which he carried dustbins. He was told one day that the rations hadn't arrived and that he would have to go to Guildford to collect them. This was just a big leg-pull but Charlie, without even knowing where Guildford was, duly set off with his cart and was only stopped when the RSM, Big 'Spike' Kelly, saw him leaving camp by the main gate. There were many others. I can remember one of our section, a big Yorkshireman named Les Wardle, asking another ex-DP, Louie the chef, for more chips. The reply was typical Louie when he told Les, 'Cheeps? I'll give you more f****** cheeps'! However, we never lacked for food in that cookhouse and Louie always gave us more when asked, even if he did have a pop at whoever was asking. Nowhere in the vast structure of the army was another camp like this one, with such an assortment of odd characters.

When not out on a task, life wasn't the usual round of military duties found in most barracks although there was one duty we had to perform, that was generally disliked; manning the guardroom switchboard! I had this only once, on a Sunday. This duty only ever devolved on us at the weekends. I was lucky in that there were no emergencies that day and I spent the whole time reading.

Stuart Ingrey told me that the only time he had to do this duty, he made a mess of it. He connected the QM to the wrong number and disconnected the CO by mistake. Few sappers were conversant with telephone switchboards and due to this, the task proved to be a difficult one.

I can remember many times when we were bored to death. After the morning parade, if there was no job on, we usually just sat around in the room. It would have been an ideal time for us to be taught something of the trade we were engaged in but the army, like God, works in mysterious ways and it was not to be.

It was at this time that we were entertained by one of the lance jacks, who was an inveterate and accomplished liar. Most units have at least one. He was a great guy in all respects, but he didn't know fact from fiction. His stories of his pre-military life included his house, his pet parrot, his sports car and all the girls who chased him. We knew it was all make-believe but we had nothing better to do. It passed a few hours. This lad also thought he could play the guitar and strummed on it incessantly. Any one of us could have told him he was wasting his time. Hank Marvin he was not!

Stu Ingrey remembers: A new subaltern arrived on the scene one day, a 2Lt Yates, quickly stuck with the nickname of 'Rowdy' after the character played by Clint Eastwood in the cowboy TV series Rawhide.

He was initiated into the Officer's Mess and was found next morning by the lads, wandering around the barrack square, hopelessly lost, confused and incapable and he was directed to his quarters. After he'd settled in, he turned out to be a good section officer.

During this time, it became apparent that Stuart was a dab hand at writing poetry. My method of passing the time was doing pencil portraits of the lads in the room. Looking back on it, we must have seemed a strange pair to the rest of the blokes, whose main considerations in life were 'beer and birds'. But, to my mind and I may have been wrong in my assumption, there was one bloke there who wasn't 100% hetero and didn't subscribe to the 'birds' part. One weekend, a gang from the unit went out on a bender and Stu Ingrey was half-carried back into the billet by a couple of them. He was helped into the NCO's bunk, the small room at one end and the door was closed. I looked over at Dave Stone and Dave nodded to me. We were obviously thinking along the same lines because we went over to the bunk, knocked on the door and picked up an unconscious Stu from the bed and took him to his own bed. We could keep an eye on him there. The lance jack whose room it was, said nothing.

We had a NAAFI in the camp, situated at the top of the square, where the offices were but it was a dingy, ill-lit, unprepossessing place, so much so that I often felt depressed drinking in there, so I often went to Horsham, where I usually drank at a pub called The Crown, which was in the town square. There was a caged monkey in the public bar that was frequently loose, and it created havoc, eating cigarettes, and drinking patron's beer. Over the other side of the square there was a Chinese restaurant, and the owner of this establishment was known to the troops as The General. I was the only one of our crowd who never ate Chinese food, labelling it 'foreign muck'.

This received a certain amount of ribald humour from my drinking partners. When they went over to eat Chinese food, I either stayed away or went with them and ate English food.

I never experienced any bad feelings from the residents of Horsham towards the army, as I did in other places in the future, and we made friends with the unlikeliest people. One night in The Crown, Scouse Gore and I got ready for the two mile hike back to camp, when two motorcycle boys in the bar asked if we wanted a lift. I asked them if they were going our way and they said they weren't, but it didn't matter and they'd run us back and save us a walk. Thinking back on it, these two had been drinking pints of bitter all evening, so we were taking a chance, but they got us safely back to camp, albeit very cold. They were wrapped up in leathers, but we had on just light jackets and trousers.

We'd seen this pair many times before but ignored them, as we did most civvies. I suppose this proved that we can't always take appearance for granted as before that, being an ex-Mod, I'd had no time for 'Rockers'. Despite their over-long hair and scruffy appearance, they were friendly enough and we drank together after that when we met in the pub.

There wasn't another cold trip on the back of a bike though. Other times we walked back to camp. A Lance Corporal Jones of our unit, lived about halfway to Horsham and often we called at his home while walking back to camp.

Ostensibly it was just a good-will call but his wife was a stunningly beautiful brunette and we really only stopped off to see her. I'm sure she knew this. She never alluded to it and was always polite and friendly to us. It was a mystery to us how that Welsh git Jones had managed to trap such a beautiful bird.

If we didn't want to make the trip to Horsham, there was always the Shelley Arms, just outside the camp and over the main road. Many's the time the lads were locked in by the publican. There, boozing was done until well after hours and as a parting gift, and a godsend in winter, milk bottles full of hot soup were given out, bottles which had to be juggled from hand to hand to prevent burns. I was never a regular patron of the Shelley, preferring the pub in town and therefore never had hot soup given to me.

Chapter Three

Bomb Disposal as we know it, was born during the dark days of the Blitz. The unit has carried on its work since then, often unnoticed. The first unexploded bombs found on British soil were recovered in the Shetland Isles. Four had been dropped at the end of 1939 but had missed their target; the seaplane moorings. Only small, they had penetrated to depths of between six and ten feet. This gave some indication of the problems anticipated by much heavier unexploded ordnance. The four small bombs hadn't been badly damaged by their impact which enabled the fuses to be extracted.

Bombs dropped blind could end up anywhere and they could not be disposed of by simply blowing them up. Fuse extraction technology would have to be designed to enable the bombs to be rendered safe. Various prototypes were constructed, some obsolete before they could be used and there was a high casualty rate among the sections tasked with disposal. At the beginning of the war, there was no provision in Britain for disposing of air-dropped ordnance, despite the fact that many knew of what was involved. Records from the Spanish Civil war indicated the Germans had gathered useful information as to the amount of damage they could do by dropping bombs on civilian targets.

They'd been in possession of air-dropped bombs, complete with electrical and impact fuses in 1931, but the Spanish Civil war gave them the opportunity to use them.

It was the Italians who first dropped aerial bombs on ground targets. These bombs were filled with nitro-glycerine. Nitro is very unstable, and the Italians were the only ones to use that filling. In The Great War, the Germans manually dropped small impact bombs from their airships and biplanes. Some were dropped on Britain. They were also used in 1917 against the Bedouin in the Middle East. So, aerial bombs weren't something new. What was new was the size. With the advent of large bombers, larger bombs could be carried. There might not be as many in a bomb load, but they did much more damage than their predecessors.

It has to be understood that bombs failing to explode on contact with the earth were not all due to fuse malfunctions or manufacturing faults.

Many were designed not to explode immediately. With a one-ton bomb possibly penetrating to thirty or thirty five feet in normal soil, the disruption caused to services and to the lives of the public all worked in the enemy's favour. The record was a bomb that was found sixty feet below ground level and it had jinked off course twice. No bombs, apart from those rudimentary First World War ones, were ever carried armed.

The method of arming varied between nations. Some bomb fuses were of the electrical condenser type. For these to explode on contact, the bombs had to be dropped from a height of more than a thousand feet. A charge would be put into the fuse as the bomb left the aircraft and when the missile struck, the shock would trigger a trembler inside, which would make contact and then explode the device.

If dropped lower than that height, the fuse wouldn't be fully charged, and the bomb would rest in the ground. On being disturbed, the trembler would activate, make contact and detonate the bomb. The addition of anti-handling devices (booby-traps) to the bomb fuses also gave the enemy an advantage. These devices were fiendish in their complexity. Lives were lost before means were found to make these safe.

The Royal Engineers were at the forefront of inventing equipment for use by the armed forces, so it was inevitable that they were also involved in trying to find solutions to the bomb fuse problem. They did. Although the original kit was very Heath Robinson, it worked. It took time to find its way to the bomb disposal teams but eventually fuse extractors, clock stoppers and other articles were in use.

In the early stages, doctor's stethoscopes were used. These were replaced by electric stethoscopes, which were much more powerful and therefore, more effective. Censorship had to be applied on the press because as soon as a piece of equipment was found to be successful, the Germans adapted their fuses to counter it, so they must have been monitoring the newspapers. From then on, little news of bomb disposal techniques, successes or failures, found its way to the general public. Editors realised that although many of the stories were of the human-interest variety, they had to be suppressed for security reasons. The less the enemy knew, the better.

Before censorship was applied, many items of bomb news were published and in the early stages of the war, there were horror stories dreamed up about the enemy. One was to the effect that a cobweb-like material had been dropped by the Luftwaffe. It was reported that an attempt to handle this had resulted in blisters. This was reported in the press, who never checked the provenance of this story. They were cobwebs! On frosty mornings, they could be seen covering the hedgerows. The report of blisters couldn't be accounted for.

One fantastic story concerned an aerial bomb that had entered the ground without exploding, had stopped and was then seen moving along under the road, shaking and bulging the road surface while moving toward the target. As will be explained later, bombs can move laterally after entering the ground and can even ricochet off, but they can't stop and then start again seeking targets.

Another story concerned a man who came home from work and found his home evacuated because of a UXB (unexploded bomb). He made the excuse to the policeman at the gate that he wanted to collect some personal items from inside. He was allowed through. While in the house, he saw a small (1 cwt) bomb sticking up out of the kitchen floor. He prised up the floorboards and got the bomb out. He then carried it out the back door, took it to the local park and dumped it. On returning to the house, he informed the copper of what he'd done. He wanted to know where his wife was, so he could go and collect her and bring her home, because he wanted his tea, and he wasn't going to cook it! I don't know whether he got his tea or not, but he did get arrested.

He was prosecuted for tampering with an enemy missile, and was a very lucky man! I wonder what the Germans thought of that report; that the English were such a phlegmatic race that they even treated enemy bombs with contempt or that some of us we were too stupid to recognise danger when it stared us in the face!

A parachute mine was dropped one night on a city in the provinces. Two ARP wardens saw it gliding in and reported it. There was no trace of it the next day. This mine was about eight feet long and two feet in diameter so it couldn't just disappear, but it apparently had done just that! Formerly all mines had been disposed of by the Navy but RE bomb disposal officers had been given permission to disarm them when necessary.

Days later, a bomb disposal team had just rendered safe two bombs in the same area, when a woman approached the officer in charge and asked him if he'd take away a piece of an aeroplane that had fallen in her backyard on the night of the raid. He told her it wasn't part of his job, but he did ask her how big this thing was. She told him it looked like part of an aeroplane body, like a large boiler. The officer and his sergeant both had the same idea, and the woman was told that they'd come along and have a look at this 'boiler'. What they found was the missing parachute mine. The homeowner, finding that this object was blocking his way to the coal shed, had built a wooden ramp over it.

He said that the ARP was so busy, he didn't want to bother them. He'd hammered nails into the structure and nothing had happened. These mines were extremely sensitive, and it was a miracle that the mine hadn't detonated. The couple were very shocked when told they'd have to leave their home while this weapon was made safe. A naval officer came to remove the fuse and while moving the mine, the clock started to tick and was gagged five seconds before detonation. Some people just could not accept that they lived in dangerous times.

Relations between the general public and bomb disposal teams were usually good but there were people who resented having the army on their property. One Essex farmer complained bitterly about broken gates, damage done to his road and the slowness of the diggers. These men had laboured for two weeks in the worst possible conditions and the farmer and his family had refused to even boil a kettle for them. The bomb was found, deep down. It was made safe and removed.

Weeks later, another bomb was reported at the same location. This was a fairly small one but it had a photo-electric cell to activate it and removal was out of the question so it was detonated in situ and all the farmhouse windows were shattered. This wasn't deliberate, just one of the hazards of enemy munitions. I would call that just retribution.

People were used to the activities of Bomb Disposal and eventually took little notice. As operations were heavily censored, all the public saw were the red-winged vehicles and the barriers and signs indicating an unexploded bomb. Most were happy enough to give the area a wide berth but there were cranks then, just as there are now. When one of these was identified, the police stepped in and took them away smartly. Some were more difficult than others. When a bomb fell on a North London cemetery, the bomb disposal team had to remove many skeletons. There were so many that they had to be stacked and propped up in the bushes nearby. During the digging, a lady approached the team because she wished to visit a grave, but she was turned away. She returned that night. The team were still working in the hole and she could hear the voices. She switched on her torch and came face to face with a rank of skeletons. She screamed and collapsed, the police were called and took her away. She risked her own life and those of the section involved. They were fighting a battle with a time-fuse.

A golf club in the north had been hit by two bombs, one of which fell on the green and the other close by. The greenkeeper decided to keep quiet about this as he didn't want anyone digging up his precious green.

All he was concerned with was this area of grass, nothing more. He filled in the entry holes and cut turf to fit the top. He was told to say nothing by the club secretary.

There was another raid some days later and this time, six bombs fell on the course. Four exploded. This time the fools had to report the matter. While the shaft was being dug to locate one of the bombs, the green keeper told the corporal that his men should be careful and not damage the greens with their muddy boots. The corporal then told the green keeper to go and f*** himself. Quite a natural reaction to a stupid suggestion.

With a fight narrowly avoided and the green keeper walking away, there was an explosion. The second bomb had detonated, not the one at the bottom of the shaft. The team, pretty much shaken up, had a break and a cup of tea and during this break, the first two bombs were mentioned. The secretary explained and the corporal said he'd now have to inform the officer in charge. They couldn't find the entry holes, because the green keeper had disguised them too well. Three shafts had to be dug before the bombs of the earlier raid could be located and made safe.

There are many strange stories concerning bombs, some barely believable. One bomb hit a railway station platform, ricocheted off the concrete and disappeared. The station and all outlying areas were searched but nothing was found. The bomb was eventually located. It had penetrated the side of a goods wagon on a passing train and come to rest there. It was discovered when the train was being off-loaded in Scotland.

Another weird story was of a bomb that hit, in February, the side of one of those huge, brick factory chimneys. The entry hole was visible, likewise the exit hole but there was no bomb. The area was minutely searched as the factory was engaged in war work, but to no effect. The bomb had indeed penetrated the chimney but instead of exiting, it had knocked bricks out of the opposite wall which made it look like an exit hole. The bomb had then fallen straight down into the base of the chimney and had not exploded. In September it detonated. The reason given was that it was extremely hot in the base of the chimney, and this had 'cooked' the bomb and brought about detonation.

The name 'doodle-bug' needs no other explanation to anyone of my age or to any member of the preceding generation but it may need explaining to younger people. It was the name given to the V1 flying bomb, the second terror weapon unleashed on Britain (the first will be described later). Just after D Day, the first ten V1's were launched. Six of these failed to reach England and the four that crossed the Channel fell in Kent. The V1 was large, about twenty five feet long and had a warhead weighing one thousand kilograms. It was simply a pilot-less plane with an engine designed to cut out at a predestined time. They flew low and at about four hundred miles per hour. One of these weapons fell on Dartmouth Park Hill in North London and obliterated many homes.

The damage covered an area of half an acre; something I know, as we kids used this bomb site as a playground in the fifties. I have no idea how many were killed and there are no people left now to ask. We lived two streets away and the shock-wave had lifted my five year old brother from the floor and slammed him down again. It also caused the partial collapse of one wall of our kitchen.

About ten thousand of these weapons were launched from ramps in occupied France and Holland and many were shot down by anti-aircraft fire or by RAF fighters and some even crash landed and it was these that gave the bomb disposal engineers examples of their fuses.

Following the V1 came the successor, the V2, Hitlers third and ultimate terror weapon. This was a rocket, the forerunner of today's missiles. Unlike the V1, which could be seen and heard, there was no warning from a V2. This thing was forty-six feet long, had a warhead weighing a ton and in flight, travelled at an amazing three thousand miles per hour and the first intimation of its presence was a huge explosion. One landed at St. Johns Way, Archway on November 5th and the area destroyed was immense. There were two hundred and fifty casualties, including thirty-five dead.

To keep information from the enemy, the V2 strikes were not admitted as such, and were reported as gas main explosions.

Prior to their launch, the V2 site at Peenemunde had been bombed by the RAF and the launch had been put back at least a year. Their arrival had been expected although there was nothing that could be done to offset it. But even these weapons were capable of failure. Four failed to explode on impact, out of one thousand one hundred and fifteen reported to have fallen on our country, but those four provided the bomb disposal men with all they needed to know about the fusing arrangement.

Obviously, when one came down and failed to detonate, it penetrated very deep. This gave rise to some extensive excavations and many weeks of work, but they were finally recovered and made safe, and their innermost secrets laid bare.

One of the first people to take on the work of disposal was Lord Suffolk. A volunteer, he attached himself to the Department of Scientific Research and was at the forefront of work involving the removal of delayed-action and other difficult fuses. With his secretary, Miss Morden, his chauffeur Mr Harts and men from the Experimental Unit, he could be found at Richmond Park, tinkering with bombs. While Lord Suffolk worked, his secretary took notes and Mr Harts helped with the instruments. It was while working on a bomb, that they, plus an NCO and four sappers were killed in May 1941 when the bomb exploded. They were all brave people and shouldn't be forgotten.

The Germans soon came to realise the potential of the bomb disposal sections and went all out to kill as many as possible with combinations of various types of fuses and anti-handling devices. Consequently, the loss rate was high. One hundred and twenty-three officers and men had been killed, with sixty-seven wounded and many of these casualties were the most experienced personnel.

The loss rate didn't deter the others engaged in this work. They had high morale, as is only natural when working as a dedicated team on a task of national importance. Strange as it may seem, working on live bombs was found to be addictive and attracted hundreds of men, although there were never enough.

To get more people into the job, the Director of Bomb Disposal agreed to accept volunteer members of what was known as the NCC (Non-Combatants Corps) otherwise known to us all as conscientious objectors, or 'conchies'. They were trained and sent to disposal sections.

Initially they were not welcomed, as they were non-combatants, wouldn't carry arms, and so couldn't be asked to act as armed guards.

Regular soldiers had to do this duty and understandably put out that the NCC members were excused. To begin with, this led to a lot of hard feelings but as time went by and the NCC members proved their worth, it was forgotten. Some members of the NCC eventually changed their views and elected to go to combat units.

This then is a small part of the background of Bomb Disposal UK. Necessary to show that from small beginnings, major advances in bomb disposal procedure came about and a unit that started with nothing, led the world in such techniques.

Chapter Four

The unit received, on average, two emergency calls per day, most of which were false alarms. This has obviously diminished with time, but it was not unusual back then for some old lady to ring and tell the police that a hole had appeared in her favourite flower bed or a man reporting that his allotment had yielded a strange metal object, pointed at one end. Munitions of many types had been uncovered in lofts and garden sheds, with instances of people using live grenades as paper-weights or shells as doorstops.

One lady called in the unit to take away from her loft three live 1kg German incendiary bombs and a 1916 hand grenade from the collection of her late husband.

In another case, a whole wall had been built of anti-tank mines and in another, a pair of live grenades had been made into candlesticks. Sadly, some of these cases were only brought to light when something went awry, detonated and killed some innocent.

One woman tried to peel the rubber from a mine and when she found she couldn't do it, she jumped on it in anger. Luckily for her it wasn't armed.

Many who kept live armaments in the home were ex-servicemen and should have known better. A shell brought back from the war and kept as a souvenir fell from a mantle-piece, exploded and killed the occupants of a room. There were many such incidents.

In 1966, 21 years after the end of the war, 15 bombs and 48 mines had been found and destroyed. Not everything reported was found to be dangerous. Many and varied was the rubbish dug up from the English Country Garden. One person reported a huge metal object which turned out to be a garden roller. How this came to be buried was a mystery.

Another strange find was a motorcycle, minus its wheels, about fifteen feet underground. We never bothered much about how these objects came to be where they were. Bike frames, mangles, tin baths, water tanks and old iron bedsteads have been found, but it's standard practice that each report has to be followed up and evaluated, just in case!

Buried bombs and dangerous munitions are still around and the object that you might think is harmless could well be a very lethal weapon. When I was a kid, the left-overs of war were all around and we thought nothing of seeing firearms and live ammunition played with in the street. The firearms were generally damaged and inoperable so presented no problem even though there should never have been access to them, but live rounds were a different proposition and one whack in the wrong place could result in death.

I had an old Mauser rifle, from the first war. I can't recall where it came from, but I do know where it ended up. I got a .303 live round jammed in the breech and my brother saw this, withdrew the bolt, and took the rifle away from me. I think Dad consigned it to a watery grave in one of the

Hampstead ponds. He'd already taken away a Webley .38 pistol from my brother, a gift from granny. That had a metal bar down the barrel and through one chamber and was bent at both ends so the gun couldn't fire but a hacksaw would have had it working in no time. Grannie's other gift to my brother was a Japanese officer's sword.

Mum hated having it in the house, so after me being nosy and cutting myself on its razor edge, she asked him to get rid of it and he sold it to a workmate for the princely sum of fifteen shillings!

That's equal now to eight pounds eighteen shillings. Even in 1954, this was a giveaway price and I hate to think what one would fetch today. Where granny got that from is a mystery because the only member of our family who fought in the far east theatre was my father and he never brought it back.

SS and SA daggers and other Nazi sidearms were commonplace. Such were the times. Weapons and munitions were everywhere!

Chapter Five

During April, we were warned for another job. Off we went to Stratford, East London. It was an area that had been devastated by the Luftwaffe and 'temporary' prefabs had been built. These prefabs had recently been vacated and the local council asked the unit to check the area as a hole had been made there during the war. Prefabs were common right through the 50's and early 60's and I can remember people living in them near Hampstead Heath. Right next door to the site was a pub called The Castle and in true East End market fashion, it opened its doors each day at 0600.

This was music to the ears of some of our more hardened drinkers. Some of the old prefabs were still standing and these housed the section. I commuted daily between the site and St. Johns Wood, where I stayed at my brother's home. I at least had a decent bed.

At first, Stuart also stayed there but we had to share a bed and with me being a nocturnal fidget, he soon gave up this idea and made his home in the prefab with the others. Before he took himself off and while still at St. Johns Wood, my brother, Stu and I went to visit my father. We walked from St. Johns Wood to the Archway. It was an enjoyable walk then. It was dad's birthday, and we took him out to his local, the Brunswick Arms, for a drink. Stuart recalls that we had a good 'knees-up' that night and were well lubricated on pints of bitter.

Much of the work done on this site was with the aid of jetting equipment. Jetting is a way of making holes in the ground using water. A small starter hole was made, followed by a pipe. Then, canvas hoses as used by the fire services, were attached by means of a fitting called a swan neck and high-pressure water was pumped down the pipe. We used a double canvas hose. When a hole had reached a certain depth, a bomb locator was lowered down the pipe and readings were taken at intervals. The readings here showed nothing unusual. A bomb would have caused magnetic anomalies, and these would have registered on the equipment's dial. Being duralumin, the jetting pipes didn't register.

Jetting is fine in normal earth but was less effective in London clay. While working this system the sergeant told me to sit on the top of the swan neck fitted at the top, to add a little weight.

A little weight is all he got as I tipped the scales at about 8 stones and a bit just then. The swan neck had a tendency to fly off due to a bad connection and once again it came off and I was hurled by the force of the water, coming through at about 350 pounds per square inch, against the side of a prefab. Although I was wearing a helmet and wet weather gear and therefore somewhat padded, I took a bang on the head. I had some other lumps and felt dizzy, so Sapper Ted D'Arcy, our Land Rover driver took me to my dad's home at the Archway, giving the neighbours something to gossip about at seeing a vehicle there with Bomb Disposal plates on front and rear. I went back to the site the next day.

The original idea of this job was merely to check if the site was safe for further development. No bomb had been reported but we laboured on and put down many holes in a grid pattern.

Contractors were driving 18-inch vertical pipes into the ground around us and when one failed to respond to pressure, Sgt F said he had a job for me. As I was the smallest, I would be lowered down the shaft, headfirst, with a rope tied around my ankles to try to find what was down there and I could then tell them what was causing the obstruction.

I couldn't believe the bloody idiot meant this. There was every chance of me getting stuck or coming across underground gas, so I refused. I knew I was on firm ground with this refusal, as it was a non-military order. Knowing he had no authority to order me to do this, he didn't push it. We didn't get on!

Living off site as I was, I missed a big fight one night. This was still the era of East End totters, and they were frequently seen in that area and they were nothing like the cosy image as presented by Steptoe and Son, of TV fame. There was great rivalry and animosity between the various totter families. Stu Ingrey said this erupted into open warfare in the Castle pub, between the Rose family and another, when hammers and knives were used. There were injuries but no deaths. It was a close thing.

After this job, it was back to camp to wait for another. We did have slack moments; it wasn't all travelling and digging.

It was during this period that I decided to go to the village of Warnham, which was within walking distance from camp. I'd been at boarding school there and had left at Christmas 1959. I wasn't exactly a model pupil so wondered what type of reception I was going to get. I'd had eighteen strokes of the cane in the year I was there. The first was because I'd thumped a lad while using a pair of home-made knuckle-dusters and when this came to light, they were confiscated.

A search was made of my belongings and other dangerous articles were uncovered and the next day, at the school assembly, the head, Ernest Savage, said he was forced due to the severity of the case to call in the local police. He did this and the local bobby said he'd leave the punishment to the head. I received six strokes and got off lightly. A short time after this, myself and another lad gave the woodwork master such grief one Saturday afternoon that he went and handed in his notice. We got six strokes for that. I can't remember what the other caning was for, although it may have been for wearing a Nazi party badge and refusing to take it off.

With this hanging over me, I put on my uniform (I wanted to show I was a reformed character) and along with Scouse Gore, who was probably itching to see me thrown off the premises, we walked the mile to the village. I remembered the way easily enough. What I didn't remember was that with it being a Saturday, it was pay parade. A similar thing to our military pay parade but without saluting. I saw the head, introduced myself and he told me he didn't recall me, so my worrying had been in vain.

He placed us into the care of two house matrons, Elspeth Macrae and Mrs Bond, both of whom I remember and both of whom remembered me. The elder of the two, Mrs. Bond recalled that she'd seen the blue stripes across my backside after my caning, when we bathed later that day.

Yes, back then, even at fourteen, we had house matrons supervising our bath night! Couldn't happen today. The girls' bath night was superintended by some very dolly house matrons but we had 'Bondie', who was elderly even in 1959. That no doubt was intended by the head, a wily old character. He knew his boys! Scouse and I were invited to tea and cakes and having spent half an hour there we bid them farewell. It was to be twenty years before I went back again.

That was the finest school of all those I'd been to and I spoilt it by acting as a hooligan. I was born in Balmore Street N19 in North London, a street renowned for villainy. Having been bought up on stories about coppers only patrolling that street in pairs and seeing different families fighting each other in the street, I was probably influenced by this.

We were a young family when mum died, and we were split up and lived with various family members in the country. Dad supposedly couldn't manage the three youngest, five, eight and ten years, me being the ten-year-old. My brother was fifteen and working so he stayed at home. After three years, I went back home and eventually found myself at boarding school.

One sister stayed with an aunt while the other also went to a boarding school. I started work in January 1960, as an engineering apprentice, although this wasn't my choice of trade.

Dad wasn't going to have me lying around the house and he took me to the local youth employment office, and it was he that chose the job for me.

I had no say in the matter. I worked at that company, learning the trade of a mechanical engineer by day and learnt about gang fights and crime during the evening, while loafing about the streets with my mates. Our venue was De Marcos café at the Archway, and we were known as The Archway Mob.

We got up to all sorts of villainy and many of the gang finally ended up in remand homes, approved schools and prisons. One even finished up as a 'lifer'. I could see where I was heading and decided to get right out of it.

I came from a military family. Both sides had been in uniform, going back to at least World War One. Mum's family were all gunners and dad's all sappers. One exception to the RA and RE rule was great uncle Claude Nunney. He was in the Canadian Expeditionary Force. Claude Stephen Sargent Nunney VC DCM MM, a real hero, died of his wounds in 1918. So, I gave it some thought and decided that it had to be the RE. It was no contest really. There was not much call in civilian life for people that knew how to fire a howitzer and I had to think of the future. I had one trade I could fall back on but wasn't sure that I wanted to devote a lifetime to it. I could sort out another trade while in uniform.

So, in July 1965, I decided to join the Royal Engineers. I hadn't given any thought to the possibility of failing to do so. REME would have been a second choice and I didn't want to be an infantryman.

I told my brother I was signing on and he came with me to the recruiting office to see fair play. He hadn't long been out of the Corps himself. The office was in Kentish Town, and we went there on a Saturday morning. I sat the aptitude test and got the required pass mark to join the RE and was told to report to Great Scotland Yard to have a medical and be sworn in. I did this a few days later, was given my shilling and a prayer book and told to report to No 1 Training Regiment, Royal Engineers on Friday 6th August 1965. Dad had hit the roof, blamed my brother for influencing me but finally accepted it.

I was asked what trade I wanted to follow and requested Fitter/Machinist. It was engineering after all. 'Fully booked', was the reply. So much for being able to pick a trade! Having one trade under my belt already, I gave up completely on engineering and opted for Bomb Disposal. An uncle had been in this unit during the last war and he, Sapper Leslie Farrow, had a very lucky day when a bomb fuse was heard to click into activation but failed to detonate the bomb. His commander remarked that he was indeed one very lucky sapper and should have died then. Knowing from experience that as a sapper, he wouldn't have been alone with that bomb, more than he would have died. He told me in later years that every day since then had been a bonus.

After entering the army, I thought I'd found why I couldn't be trained as a Fitter/Machinist; people from most of the depressed areas of Britain were in the Corps and had snapped up these trades. I did sit and pass two painter and decorator courses at later dates, securing a City and Guilds of London certificate because along with gunners, there weren't many openings for bomb disposal engineers out there either.

There wasn't much time off between the Stratford job and the next, which was a real change. It was summer, the task was in Sussex, and we commuted daily. A schoolteacher, Mrs. Patricia Woolard had been murdered on the Bognor to Victoria train and the murder weapon, a knife, was unaccounted for. We went to common land at Ifield, near Crawley and used mine detectors in an unsuccessful search for this weapon.

While searching the fields, I came across an old camp hidden in the trees and there, next to a pile of cold ashes, I did in fact find a knife, a table knife that had been ground down to a Bowie blade shape.

I called the nearest policeman, who looked at the knife and said it wasn't what they were looking for. (I hope to this day that he was right!) When it became apparent that the murder weapon wasn't going to be found, the police put on a show for us. They had dogs with them, big Alsatians, used to bring down criminals. I volunteered to be fitted with a sleeve and I was told to run. The dog was released and grabbed my right arm and I was whirled round and thrown down and the dog stood over me, a dog with huge teeth. I was told to keep still and was more than happy to comply. These dogs were totally different from the war dogs we had back in camp. They would never have just stood over anyone. They were killers and they'd have gone for the throat and sunk their teeth in.

It was a break from ordinary tasking; just a pity that we were there because a young woman had been brutally murdered. While I was away on the hunt for a murder weapon, my mate Stuart Ingrey went off and got married. I would like to have been there but we were on different gangs and working far apart. He invited the gang he was working with at the time and the ceremony was performed at his local church on 4 June. It all went off smoothly and the happy couple were photographed outside the church, with Stu in topper and tails and looking very different from the usual scruff-order in which he normally appeared. It was to be four years before I was to meet his wife, Sarah. She's been a good friend since.

Once a year we had to devote time to real spit and polish. This was for Admin Parade. Rooms were dusted, floors polished and general housekeeping undertaken but to a level unheard of in the average home. Living in wooden huts that had no proper ceiling, we had to clamber up onto the roof beams to dust them off, (just as we had to do while in training regiment). We knew this would be a place that would be looked at. They always checked this area out, assuming, I suppose that being high, we'd not bother to clean it.

Prior to the main inspection, Sgt F checked the room and once again he and I didn't see eye to eye. He was inspecting the floors and they gleamed! But he was out to find fault with me, come what may, and he did. He picked up a chair and looked at the bottom of each leg. Having been moved about on the floor, the legs had collected some polish and to this, a little fluff had stuck. He went ballistic and said it was disgusting and filthy and I was to get it cleaned up. I was waiting for him to get more personal, but he didn't. (An old friend of mine from that same unit said to me recently that he never liked Sgt F but if he met him today, he'd buy him a pint. Well, I wouldn't!)

Admin also meant a full-dress parade on the square. This was the only unit I saw that had Sterling SMG's as everyone's personal weapon. We therefore had to practice Sterling arm's drill. A very easy drill and it was impressive to see so many in the parade carrying this firearm. I can't remember who inspected us that day, but it was a General Officer.

We marched round the camp and onto the square and did the usual arms drill, a march past in review order and presenting arms. There had been no real saluting base on the camp, so we had to build one beforehand and paint it and the ropes a blinding white. George Cooney was resplendent in as many medals as he thought safe to wear and it was the only time in that unit that we paraded in full uniform. The CO, Lt. Col. Townsend-Rose, affectionately known as Guy Fawkes or alternatively, 'Timson-Thomson' Townsend-Rose and half-brother to Princess Margaret's old boyfriend, Peter Townsend, was in attendance, along with our other officers, the RSM, and two WO2's, Morshead and Murphy.

No one had thought to get 'Wings', the Corps march for the parade so we marched to a Royal Artillery tune, The Voice of the Guns, played on a record player and rigged up to speakers. Everything very ad hoc but it was a brave turn-out. It's usual at this time to have a BFT, a Basic Fitness Test, including assault course and ranges to assess a unit's efficiency. We classified with our SMG's at Kithurst Ranges, at thirty, one hundred and two hundred yards and fired the Webley .38 pistol but this was more for fun. It was generally reckoned to be a good day out. Range days were one of life's better times, providing you weren't one of the unfortunates working in the butts and I loved the feel of that weapon in my hands. After classifying, we shot at empty boxes on the range, just for fun.

The Sterling was a fine SMG, light and easy to strip down and maintain and only let down sometimes by inferior ammunition. Bad ammo meant each round had to be pushed into the breech individually as there was not enough gas to re-cock the weapon. Imagine that happening in a war situation! We had a make-shift assault course, where Tim Vismer, on a rope suspended between two cranes, fell and broke his arm, so not such a good day out for him!

This BFT was nothing like the standard ones that I did later. The normal BFT was a forced march of ten miles, wearing fighting order webbing, steel helmet and carrying a personal weapon. This was followed by jumping a nine-foot ditch, climbing two walls, one of six feet and one of twelve feet, carrying a comrade, his kit and weapon one hundred yards (he carried you back!) and ended by firing on the range (and hitting the target!)

The march took one hour and fifty minutes and the whole test, two hours and yes, it can be done, as any soldier or ex–soldier will tell you. The incentive to pass was not having to do it all again, generally the next day, if we failed to complete it in the required time.

Chapter Six

We had another task during that grand summer of 1966, and this took us to the by-lanes of Surrey. An elderly man, a professor, had belatedly reported (twenty-five years belatedly in fact!) that a bomb had fallen in his garden during the war years.

He found the bomb's tail fin near the entry hole but had failed to report it, something he should have done immediately. He had thought nothing of it at the time and had filled in the entry hole and forgotten about it, but his conscience had been pricked by the advice of a friend, a Civil Defence worker and he'd made a report. The homeowner was a Mr. William Potter and as mentioned, he was a professor. What his discipline was, I don't know but it certainly wasn't in cleanliness or good order. He was the archetypal scatty professor, serious faced, with unkempt clothes, almost bald and with what hair he had sticking out at all angles. On his kitchen table he had a partially dismantled car engine, and the place was a tip. His wife, probably used to the disorder, worked around this.

We arrived in West Ewell, near Epsom, in July. This time we'd been billeted in the Epsom TA Centre, sleeping on camp beds, therefore no subsistence pay! The site where we had to work was in Chessington Road, a good location, a tree-lined side road, off the main thoroughfare. There were fields and hedgerows nearby and it was very rural. Being summer, the sun shone, flowers were in bloom, trees were in full leaf and we could have been in worse places. Having once lived in a Buckinghamshire village, I felt very much at home. Such a change from the earlier jobs and the rigours of winter. We unloaded our kit and made ready to start work.

While this was being done, others began to clear the garden, which resembled a jungle. It was going to look much worse in the days to come. First came the jetting to see if we could locate a bomb. This proved inconclusive. The homeowner showed us where the bomb was supposed to have struck and it was decided that a shaft would have to go down. A shaft template, made from scaffolding planks, was put together on the road and then put in place. The shaft was started with little trouble but it soon became apparent that we were going to have to cut through water pipes and the sewage system.

This was carried out and the water pipe was diverted to the house. The sewage pipe was a different matter. We had no means of capping this or diverting it. We had no tank with us capable of containing the contents, so a mud plug was rammed into the end of the pipe and all were warned about the dangers of flushing the toilet. It worked until I left the site for three days. The section and the house owners had been using the toilet but not flushing it so a big 'log jam' had built up in the pipe.

The day I rejoined the section, I used the toilet, totally forgetting about the plugged pipe. I flushed the toilet, the plug shot out and Les Wardle, who was the only one in the hole at the time, got the lot on the back of the neck. Les, reeking, with toilet paper and other muck plastered on him, came out of that shaft almost without touching the sides. Covered in glory he was not, and I beat a hasty retreat. He was normally docile, but that day he'd left his placid self behind and was hell-bent on murder. A couple of the lads quietened him down and I did the best thing possible, I got in the shaft and cleaned it up. Les was OK later, especially after I'd bought him a couple of pints.

After this incident, an Elsan toilet was installed and everyone used that but one day, a strange driver arrived on site to deliver goods and knowing no different, he used and flushed the inside toilet. Stu Ingrey and I were taking our turn in the shaft. Due to the depth we'd reached, we all wore miner's helmets while in the shaft. We'd discarded our shirts due to the heat.

When the driver flushed the toilet, Stu recalls that he heard a hissing sound which made him immediately think of a camouflet but it was the sound of water coming through under pressure. The mud plug blocking the sewage pipe flew the width of the shaft and Stu and I were covered in crap and stale urine. Stu said what he remembers most was the soiled and soggy pieces of toilet paper hanging from the peak of my helmet and the look of disbelief, then outrage on my face.

We came out of the shaft and went looking for the driver but he'd long gone. We cleaned up back at the TA Centre.

I can remember just a little of this. I ought to recall more of it as I was one of the central figures.

Having the military in West Ewell was something of a novelty and we attracted a lot of attention, not only from the locals but from all sorts of traveling salesman and even gypsies, all intent on selling us something. I did buy some black towels from a pukka salesman which looked great but when used, left me covered in black fibres. I forgot to wash them first.

People would stop and watch what we were doing in their leafy backwater. The last thing they thought of was a 25-year-old bomb near their homes. They were going to be apprised of this fact a bit later.

We spent some weeks digging there and one Friday lunchtime, when we were looking forward to going to the post office to draw our pay, our sergeant told us that we had to carry on working and the pay would be collected the following week. This meant we had seven more days without cash, and we told him that we needed money. He refused to listen, so we did a really stupid thing, we downed tools! We told him 'no money, no work'.

He was incandescent. He asked us did we think we were bloody civilians that we thought we could down tools.

He reminded us that we'd sworn an oath of allegiance and finished up by threatening us with instant jail at the Guards Depot in Pirbright followed by multiple courts martial for mutiny. He grilled Scouse McGeachin as to whether he'd had anything to do with this or if he agreed with it, at which Scouse had to say he didn't. I don't know who talked the sergeant round, but I suspect it was George Cooney and he gave in, albeit with bad grace and we went and collected our cash but he made it plain to us that he thought we were a useless bunch who didn't deserve to be called sappers and we were warned about our future behaviour.

It wouldn't have taken much for Sgt F to have charged us all and we'd have stood no chance at a court martial. In the discipline aspect he was in the right for once. The same can't be said for his attitude to his team being without cash for a week. I must add that only two didn't throw in their lot with us and they were our section Lance Corporal, Ian McGeachin and George Cooney. As Junior NCO's they dared not!

I found later that this wasn't the only time that Sgt F had attempted to implement fortnightly pay, with the same result. With his rank, he could afford to do this, but we were on a much lower rate of pay and needed our money weekly.

The first instance was on the Stratford job, where he again threatened the team with court martial for mutiny and it was Stu Ingrey that he finally picked on, telling him to step outside, his intention being either to beat Stu up or more likely, to let Stu hit him so he could charge him with striking an NCO.

If he chose the first course of action, he would kiss goodbye to his stripes because there were witnesses and there was no way it would have been kept quiet. Anyway, he was interrupted and told Stuart to f*** off and get back to work.

Sgt F had no idea of man management. His answer to every vexing problem was bullying and threats. Jim Slack, another of the sergeants, used to stop work at midday on payday, go to the post office where his team cashed their postal orders and then go to the local pub. No work was done that afternoon. His team worked like Trojans, knowing their efforts were appreciated and that they'd be paid every week.

It was a glorious 'shirts off' summer and making the most of it, we all had a reasonable tan. No one knew then of the dangers of ultraviolet rays and skin cancer. Once again, we were digging in clay and our progress in

Jetting
L-R Sappers Eden, Gore & Vismer, LCpl McGeachin

Making the template
L-R Sgt F., LCpl McGeachin, Sappers Gore, Wardle,
Farrow. Hutton, our driver, looking on

the shaft wasn't spectacular and only really improved when Les Wardle was digging. We had two types of shovel, the shovel GS and the shovel RE. Being small, I opted for the smaller GS version but when Les got in the shaft, he'd throw the GS shovel aside and tell us that he couldn't use this f****** teaspoon and to give him a man-sized shovel. We were happy to oblige and while we watched, Les would dig away to his heart's content with his RE shovel.

The shaft was taken down to about fifteen feet and periodic checks were made of the bottom and sides by a bomb locator, without success.

Time off was spent drinking in Epsom or in various local pubs. While in an Epsom pub one night, Tony Eden and I bumped into a minor pop star, who called herself 'Twinkle' and when I say bumped, I mean just that. She was most put out and told us to watch what we were doing and be more careful and then, with her nose in the air, she asked us if we knew who she was. We hadn't a clue and didn't care either and told her so. She said that her name was Twinkle. I told her I was Sparkle and Eden followed it up by saying that he was the fairy godmother. What a silly cow that girl was!

Toward the end of the job, a big booze-up was held in the TA Centre bar and me and Stu Ingrey, who had by this time joined us from another stretch at Dungeness, declining the pints of bitter that the others were drinking, instead drank Bloody Mary's and we polished off at least one full bottle of vodka between us. To say we were incapable of anything constructive the next day is a masterly understatement. All I wanted to do was find somewhere cool and dark to die.

We had to suffer the lash of Sgt F's tongue but this time it was well-deserved and he could have made things very tough for us if he'd wanted to. Our mistake was, we were beer men, first and foremost and drinking spirits was something we rarely did.

Stu probably needed to relax after his last task. The section there had recovered a lot of unexploded ammunition, including three-inch Naval shells and Stu had been narrowly missed by a lump of hot shrapnel that came winging in. Where the shrapnel could have come from, I have no idea because Dungeness Point was no longer being used as a naval gunnery range and a new power station was to be built there, hence the clearance task.

Along with the sappers, there were two civvies working in that section. The section had been working at

Dungeness but had been diverted to look for mines on the Dover/Canterbury Road. Contractors were widening the carriageway when they found an anti-rank mine. Work was stopped until the section arrived. Six more mines were found, using 4C mine detectors. There was no record of these mines and no one knows who laid them but they were a legacy of 1940 and the expected German invasion. One of the civvies was an Aussie called Roy; bush-hatted and getting on in years. He carried a .410 shotgun around with him and supplied items for the pot. Another was Derek Pearson. As explained, there was a strange hotchpotch of people working in that unit. Nowhere else in the British army could civvies and soldiers work and live so closely together. For one thing, the average civilian showed no inclination to understand or tolerate the military and most soldiers had very little or no respect for civilians at all, apart from those who'd already 'done their bit'.

The 'Tommy this and Tommy that' attitude hadn't changed much from days gone by and we all knew it and acted accordingly. Before acceptance, a civilian had to prove his worth to us and they did.

A 50kg bomb was eventually discovered slightly outside the shaft. In pouring rain and with the local residents evacuated, the fuse was extracted, and was made safe. At least, that's the official story. The unofficial one is totally different. No bomb was found. The duty driver went back to Broadbridge Heath at night and collected an empty bomb case and brought it back to the site. Then, during the hours of darkness, the timbers were lifted at one side of the shaft, the bomb was dug into the earth and the timbers let down. Next day, the bomb was 'found'. I have it on good authority that the bomb didn't look as if it had just spent 25 years underground. It was painted green, just as the practice bombs were that we used.

The decision to do this couldn't have been made at our level, although planting the bomb was. Sgt F is exonerated from the decision making but would have had to be the one who put the bomb into the ground. The ultimate decision for all of this would have had to be a very senior one.

Why it was decided to do it may be due to the man-hours spent, the expense and the disruption caused. The homeowner said he picked up a tail fin, so presumably a bomb had struck nearby. And if there was a bomb, where did it go? Is it still entombed under the road or is it resting under a neighbour's greenhouse? I wouldn't have included this as I think it demeans a great unit but as I'm trying to be honest about what I saw and did, I must record it.

This book is factual, 'warts and all', as the saying goes. One other and myself know what happened at the end of that job. I'll leave it to anyone that may read this book to form their own opinion about it.

After this, the site was then cleared of all our equipment, shaft timbers were taken apart, cleaned off and loaded, jetting kit dismantled and the thousand and one small jobs done that would leave the place as tidy as possible. Nothing could disguise the area where we'd been digging; only time would heal that, with new growth. The garden hadn't been much to look at before we started work so we hadn't made a great deal of difference to it. Then it was back to Broadbridge Heath and wait to see what delights the Luftwaffe had left for us elsewhere.

Prior to this, of course, was the big clean-up that followed every job. Everything had to be stripped down and where possible, washed down, but this was no hardship in the summer. During winter, splashing about in water that's a few degrees above freezing is not my idea of fun; fingers aching and face raw from the cold. But, being July, the winter was a thing of the past and we had sunshine and could even enjoy cleaning down the kit.

It must have been about this time that we went on leave. We sorted out our kit and had the room looking good for inspection and then we had pay parade. Just after the parade, one of the lads in the room said his wallet was missing.

A big search was made through the rooms and the toilets but with no result. So, a locker search was made. Nothing was found and no one expected a result. It was decided after a 'Chinese parliament' that we'd all chip in and make up the forty pounds that he said he'd lost. I won't mention any names but to this day, I'm sure that his money wasn't lost or stolen, and he was just out to get more. He took us for a ride, and we fell for it but it was that sort of unit, in that the blokes would help each other if in difficulties. Still, one would need a very 'brass neck' to take advantage in this way and, had he been found out, his health and safety expectancy would have been numbered in seconds.

During the early part of August, three policemen had been shot dead near Wormwood Scrubs in London and the unit was asked to sweep the area with mine detectors in a search for weapons. As the unit was in the middle of moving from Broadbridge Heath to Chattenden, in Kent, No1 troop from Brackenbury Barracks at Felixstowe, who were on beach minefield clearance, supplied the personnel for that job. They had No1 section working at Scarborough, No2 at Felixstowe and No3 at Mundesley. It was possibly a real break for them from their usual labours.

**Cpl Ken Summers (left) and team,
in the rain, sweeping the beach for mines**
Westward Ho

Beach minefield clearance was one of the worst jobs. The mines, mostly laid in haste in 1940, were to counter the expected German invasion and during the intervening years, they'd not only deteriorated, but many had also moved.

Minefields should be logged and each mine recorded, as the enemy cannot be guaranteed to detonate the mines with his armour and he who lays the mines, may well have to remove them later. Mines were laid in beaches, marshes, estuaries and mud flats, woods and even golf courses. Those laid on beaches were the worst as they were often in unstable sand and pebbles. Many were inexpertly recorded and some not at all. Some, the tide shifted about. In 1943, when it became apparent that the Germans weren't going to be wandering about on our beaches after all, an effort was made to trace and remove them, but cliffs had collapsed on some and sand dunes had built up over others. The B-type-C mine was without doubt the worst mine of all to deal with. Thousands were lifted but it was and still remains, a miserable, tedious and dangerous task, not helped by the weather.

It was invariably raining while on this work. I didn't envy those tasked for it. It was the worst possible part of Bomb Disposal as it took up more resources and personnel than any other aspect of the job. A big problem was the local councils, who didn't see why their beaches and beauty spots should be closed in the holiday season. They argued that after all this time, the mines represented no danger, had rotted away or had been damaged by damp.

They gave no co-operation or assistance at all to the units tasked with mine removal and in many cases were downright obstructionist.

People began to believe the nonsense put out and disregarded the warning notices, until lives were lost. Mines don't rot, they deteriorate, which makes them more dangerous and they had to be lifted and destroyed. Those employed on mine disposal didn't expect anything in the way of recognition but they surely could have hoped for a little understanding from the very local authorities they were trying to help.

The term Bomb Disposal has passed into history. Now, the unit is called Explosive Ordnance Disposal, or EOD. No longer are trucks seen with their distinctive red front wings.

Today's vehicles are white vans with Bomb Disposal in small, black lettering. When we served, we rode about in 3-ton trucks, with large Bomb Disposal notices, red on white, on front and rear. It was always good to drive through a large town. If we were fortunate to travel through at lunchtime, girls would be waving at us as we passed by, some blowing kisses. This was especially the case in London. Once travelling along the M1 motorway, an open top sports car came up behind us with a real dolly driving. To me, she looked like a model. We hung over the tailboard, waving at her. She was momentarily held up by traffic but indicated right, blew us a kiss, and overtook. That can't happen to anyone in the back of one of today's white vans! These episodes helped to lighten the load a bit and made me feel special and somewhat made up for the lousy times we had while wrestling with timbers for a shaft, getting a recalcitrant pump to work in the rain or stumbling about the bottom of a shaft with freezing sleet coming down our collars and numbing our hands and ears. But we'd volunteered for this job so had no one to blame but ourselves for any hardship.

Arriving at Broadbridge Heath Camp,
a unit 3-ton truck of the 60's,
instantly recognisable throughout Britain.
This one had no blue light or Bomb Disposal signs

We were issued with an arm badge, a scarlet oval, depicting a gold bomb, with two blue stripes around the nose. The badge, worn on the lower left sleeve, had been approved by King George VI during December 1940. The late Queen Mary had even been involved in the design. It was issued to all ranks and set us apart from other units. To the best of my knowledge, there was no other badge like it in the army.

Few had one and I wore mine for most of my service and wore it with immense pride. Because I was no longer serving with that unit, I was ordered to remove it from my tunic within a few months of my discharge by a nit-picking Sgt Major, for which he got no thanks from me and the one black mark against him from my point of view. The later issue versions of this arm badge were smaller, khaki and very inferior looking.

On the 6th of August, the unit moved to Lodge Hill, near Chatham and the complete move took just four days. It was a monumental task but was done successfully with a minimum of fuss. Because the unit was an operational one, fully committed to the destruction of dangerous hardware, no one was recalled to help with the move.

No jobs were postponed or cancelled and those remaining in camp had to manage as best they could. The boys from Christ's Hospital came along and did what they could. So, after 16 years, the people of Broadbridge Heath said goodbye to the unit, along with the bombs from Bomb Alley and all the things that the locals had come to see on unit open days. This move wasn't anticipated with any enthusiasm by us, the soldiers. We knew that our days of isolation were now over. We were going to a proper regiment, one with a Regimental Sergeant Major totally unlike our own Spike Kelly, and all the paraphernalia of parades, barrack squares and square bashing, saluting and other, to us, quite unnecessary military rubbish.

I took no part in the unit move; I was working but can't recall where. I did end up working with Lance corporal Dave Stone, in Hampshire. Dave had taken an active part in the move so it must have been after that occurrence.

The Hampshire task was to check for unexploded ordnance at Barton Stacey Camp, then the home of the RE Survey Regiment but in the past had been a battle training area. We found a lot of small items, much of it still dangerous. I enjoyed working with Dave. He came from Sidlesham in Sussex. He was invariably happy, never rank conscious and we hit it off well. He'd served in the Radfan, on Operation Nutcracker, was a Bomb Disposal Engineer B2 and had been around, as the 239, the first three digits of his army number implied, so I felt in safe hands. His normal sphere of operations was Battle Area Clearance.

It was a glorious job, much of it grubbing around fields and hedgerows in the sun during the day and drinking with the Ukrainians in Tilshead during the evening. Westdown Camp, Tilshead had been home to the Ukrainians for years and they had built up an independent unit there. I understood nothing of what they said and few of them could speak much English, but they took me under their wing. The food there was just as good as that at Broadbridge Heath and just as plentiful. As I was small and thin, they obviously thought I needed building up. There was a lot of pork eaten; pork, potatoes and cabbage featuring almost daily on the menu. This was another camp composed of spiders, wooden buildings resting on short concrete pillars.

Tilshead village had a pub, called the Black Horse. The landlord was a Londoner named Bill Foster and while talking to him, I found that he'd owned the local pet shop on Dartmouth Park Hill, just round the corner from where I was born. I remembered it well, although I'd never shopped there.

It was practice among the Ukrainians drinking in the Black Horse to settle who paid for the round by one of their number presenting a one pound note and someone guessing 'odds or evens' as to the final digit on the note's serial number. Get it wrong and you paid! It was fairly foolproof. Dave and I went to Salisbury one day and spent time drinking in one of the pubs and there, we pledged brotherhood. Not something silly like cutting ourselves and being made blood brothers but the next best thing, I suppose. We've been friends ever since.

DAVE STONE

Dave enlisted in the Royal Engineers on the 8th November 1962 and reported to No 1 Training Regiment on the 19th, for eighteen weeks of training. His first posting after pass-off was to 12 Field Squadron at Ripon, Yorkshire. One of the detachments from there was to Ullswater, where he helped build a jetty for the Duke of Edinburgh's Adventure Centre. The jetty was prefabricated, like a Meccano set and the pieces were bolted together. Some diving was necessary, to drive the metal sections about three feet into the bed of the lake.

Another detachment he was on was to St. Kilda. St. Kilda is an island forty miles west of the Outer Hebrides and the project was to improve the water level at a landing stage so fishermen could moor their boats. Heavy equipment was needed to shift rock and some blasting had to be done. At Oban, all the equipment was loaded onto a landing craft, which then set off. As the landing craft approached Benbecula, strong winds started to blow, which increased to gale force and the captain of the vessel took shelter at the island. Next morning the seas had moderated and although the wind was still strong, the gale had abated, allowing the craft to set off again.

At St. Kilda, plastic explosives were bound to steel matting and placed in position. At high tide, the explosives were detonated and the rock cracked open, enabling the rubble to be removed. This job took about one month.

On the 15th October 1963, the squadron landed at RAF Khormaksar, Aden and was transferred to Falaise Camp, Little Aden. Their task was to work on three Twynham hut sites at Anzio. The site had to be levelled and laid for concrete bases. On the 4th January 1964, the job came to a halt and 2 Troop moved up country into the Yemen, 'Wolves of Radfan' territory. This was 'Operation Nutcracker' and the task took on new dimensions. There was a road to be built through rough, rocky terrain, so armoured vehicles and heavy guns could be moved up. Rocks blocking the route had to be blasted.

The 'Red Wolves' were armed with new weaponry by the Russians, with rifles, ammunition and grenades. An Arab battalion was on standby while work was done on the road. In the heart of enemy territory, with adrenalin pumping, an attack was expected at all times. Moving rocks had to be done

Cpl Dave Stone

with extreme caution, for fear of booby-traps or scorpions.

Supplies were brought in by RAF helicopters. Pioneer transport and Navy Wessex helicopters from the aircraft carrier HMS Centaur, in Aden harbour helped with the airlift. Hawker Hunter jet fighters flew and fired on sniper positions. 2 Troop came off the road on the 28th February and returned to Falaise. Work started again at Anzio and Dave drove a dump truck until 16th September and he returned to the UK on the 17th and went on a trade training course, after having a well-earned twenty-four days leave. For campaign service, he was awarded the GSM 1962 with RADFAN clasp.

His next posting was to BAOR, with 12 Field Squadron at Osnabruck. He boxed there as a light heavy, fighting for the regiment and winning one fight and losing another on a TKO. He also joined the tug of war team and they narrowly lost third position. After that he was on exercise with NATO troops, preparing an iron bridge for demolition, building a Bailey bridge and a pontoon bridge over the Weser.

He returned to the UK and joined 49 Bomb Disposal Squadron on the 19th November 1965, after completing a Bomb Disposal Class 2 trade test. He was then posted to Storrington to help supervise Ukrainian teams on Battle Area Clearance. In 1966 he worked mainly on clearance tasks. One was at Devil's Dyke, a National Trust area. Another was at Yapton, known as The Jungle, because so much undergrowth needed to be removed before detection work could begin. Dave moved down To Westdown Camp at Tilshead and joined the Ukrainian team for work on Salisbury Plain. He worked at the School of Survey on range clearance. He said it was high summer and a very enjoyable time.

Chapter Seven

I spent about a week at Tilshead and then, at the beginning of September, I was whisked away to Larkhill, on Salisbury Plain, to help 'Taff' Vowels, one of our plant operators, with his job of back-blading the Plain, flattening the ground and exposing any left-over dangerous ordnance. There were invariably two men at least on each job, for safety reasons. We operated in an armoured D7 bulldozer and the din in that confined space was dreadful. However, being cooped up in there was necessary. We ran over smoke mortars, which ignited and choked us with clouds of foul smoke, but it could have been something more lethal.

One night, Taff went to see someone at a different part of Larkhill Camp, and I tagged along. We came to an open window in a well-lit kitchen and Taff spoke to a cook who was labouring away, cutting meat. He was asked if he was on night shift and he told us he wasn't, he was going home just as soon as he'd cut up the steaks to take back to his house. No wonder we ate such bloody rubbish when the cooks were taking the best cuts home with them. I asked Taff what he was going to do about this, him being a lance jack; he replied that he wasn't going to do anything at all. Typical bloody NCO! That was a short duration job, lasting only about three days, after which I returned to camp but to a totally different set-up than the one I'd left.

My first port of call was Kitchener Barracks, a Georgian edifice and one well hated by generations of Royal Engineers. The emphasis here was on 'bull' and the Colonel took the morning parade on horseback. We watched prisoners scrubbing down tables and bulling the cannon mounted outside the guardroom. I recall my brother telling me about the time he was in 'close tack' in these very barracks. Not a good experience apparently.

Our accommodation was on the second floor and consisted of long, grim barrack rooms. The food was bad too. Chattenden couldn't be worse than this – could it? Chattenden Barracks wasn't worse as far as accommodation was concerned but it was a far cry from the twenty-man rooms at the last camp. It was good but had no character, just small boxes where we could rest our weary heads. The food was no better than that served up at Kitchener. No more Big Louie cooking for us, no more extra chips, just army cooks from the ACC, also known as Andy Capp's Commandos or the Aldershot Concrete Company and any ex- soldier will tell you what that was like!

Sometime later in September we were tasked to go to Bristol. This time it was working in a school playground. Someone had reported bombs falling in that area during the bombing of that city and it was decided to check this report out. It must have been logged as wartime low priority or the unit would have been called in years before. Once again it was a B&B for us, at good digs in Brislington but this time there was no alternative hidey-hole to creep off to so we all paid up and enjoyed proper accommodation. I got so cosy there, the landlady brought me tea in bed on some nights. Just tea!

I spent a lot of time there stringing along with Bernie 'Sailor' Roome, so called because he'd served as a boy sailor before joining man-service in the army. We were often the only two of the section that stayed behind of a weekend. We enjoyed a couple of pints of an evening, without getting paralytic.

This was yet another jetting job. The tarmac in the playground had to be drilled out before we could use the jetting equipment and when this was accomplished, we started trying to get the pipes in the ground. This job also took weeks and was boring. Also, the weather had changed, and it was often raining and decidedly cooler than before. Again, we drew a blank and found no bomb within the parameters of our search area.

The reporting of unexploded bombs during the war had been very haphazard. Some had been reported in the wrong location and some had been reported when there was no bomb at all. It's understandable that while under attack, the civilian population was often confused.

However, records did exist of many bomb strikes and all had to be proved or otherwise. One problem facing future bomb disposers was the lack of suitable records and a lack of coordination during the war between different departments of the civil authority. Some bombs were double reported and some not reported at all due to one section of authority thinking that another had reported it and vice versa. This continued until a cohesive, centralised method of reporting was devised which encompassed all sections of the civil authority. And the fact that this was all new was something to be overcome. It was learning on the job!

Many a bomb, on striking the ground, failed to penetrate, and shot off at a tangent and others, when entering the ground, changed direction and travelled parallel to the surface for some distance. So, until someone could prove in the future the existence of a device, we had to assume after our negative search that this bomb didn't exist but was a reporting mistake.

A task that came up in 1966 which I wasn't involved in was the Hammersmith job. How the existence of the bomb was known is lost in the mists of time, but it must have been recorded somewhere. Apart from the enclosed photo, taken from a newspaper article, I could find no records of that bomb available today. A huge coffer dam was erected in the Thames to enable the sappers to get down to the bomb, which was close to one of the bridge abutments. Pumps were working constantly but despite this the men had to wear Admiralty pattern dry suits.

John Green can't recall if it was early morning or late at night but it was still dark. He was standing on the cofferdam walkway, hauling up a sump bucket filled with water. This was a heavy piece of equipment. While he was doing this, along came Les Wardle. In his thick Yorkshire accent, he asked John if he was having trouble and obviously unaware of what was on the other end, grabbed the rope. John let go and the weight of the dropping bucket flipped Les over the side of the cofferdam into the Thames. He was rescued and brought back to dry land, none the worse for wear. That bucket was a ten

LCpl John Green, marked x, at the bottom of the coffer dam
Hammersmith 1966

gallon one, heavy even empty. As John pointed out, one gallon of water weighs ten pounds. Ten gallons weighs one hundred pounds, so 'gravity does work!'

It was a cold, wet, miserable task, made worse by the tidal conditions. A bomb was located and made safe. I've included this report to show the conditions we sometimes had to work in. Sewage farms, cemeteries, rivers, mud flats, railway tunnels, back gardens, school playgrounds and gasworks were all grist to our mill. Jerry didn't differentiate on where he dropped his bombs and one target was as good as another to him, although this one was no doubt a deliberate attempt to destroy the bridge. Saturation bombing meant just that and many of those bombs were designed NOT to explode on contact.

Also, if a plane couldn't reach the target area, no pilot was going to return with a bomb load, so the bombs were dropped at random. Being enemy territory, the bombs might still create havoc, no matter where they were dropped. The Hammersmith bomb and Great Yarmouth bomb recently recovered (Feb 2023) from the river Yare and thousands like them don't come into the random category, as they were intended for bridges and harbour installations. Most have been recovered but some are still buried deep and are still lethal, as shown when the 250kg Yarmouth bomb detonated while being made safe.

Chapter Eight

If the past jobs I'd been on were sometimes non-productive, the next one more than made up for them. It was on a Friday night, and everyone had left for home, there being no jobs lined up. I decided to stay back and catch a later train to avoid the crush. Big mistake! I was getting changed into civvies when Mick Scott, the duty driver charged in, looked around and told me to get changed back into uniform as there was a crash call. Wonderful, and me just about to leave and no one else in the bloody building. The normal requirement was four sappers.

So, swearing like a trooper, I got changed back into working kit and went with Mick down to the duty Land Rover. It was permanently kitted out for just such an emergency. There was the Troop OC, Captain Brian Dace, known as BD, and Lieutenant Young. Just the four of us.

We set off for places unknown and then it started to rain. We headed in the direction of London, and we had no escort. We often had police outriders but not this time and the OC was cursing because cars were not moving out of our path, even though we had the blue lamp flashing. Bomb Disposal vehicles at that time were very distinctive, red painted front wings, blue flashing lights and front and rear bomb disposal plates, red letters on white. But it was dark, the rain was lashing down, and I doubt if any other driver would have seen that it was a military vehicle, let alone one on an emergency run.

When we reached our destination, it was obvious why we didn't get a free path. There was a small hole right through the middle of the blue light, probably caused by a stone from a vehicle in front and it had broken the bulb. There was a bell on our vehicles, but they were seldom used, normally only if we had a police escort.

We arrived at Beddington, Croydon. By this time the rain was, if anything, even worse and we were wearing just combat kit so before long we were all soaked.

Just before knocking off time, an excavator bucket had hit something metallic and on closer inspection, the operator didn't like the look of whatever his machine had hit. It looked suspiciously like a bomb and a phone call was made to the local police, who called in the unit. They police would have inspected the object, and also not liked the look of it and evacuated the immediate area in anticipation.

The smaller German bombs, 50–500kg, were described by weight and then given the letters SC or SD. The larger and therefore the worst bombs had nicknames, Satan, Esau, Fritz and Hermann, this one was a Hermann, presumably named after the fat Reichsmarshall. While it didn't match up to Fritz's 3,200 pounds and was far below the destructive power of Satan's 4,000 pounds it was 2,400 very unfriendly pounds of metal and high explosive.

This type of bomb had only one fuse, which was normally an impact one but clockwork fuses weren't unknown.

Clockwork fuses had in the past been found to have jammed (but still operational) and no one could say just how long there was left on the clock if and when it started up again. This one had been hit by an excavator so there was no telling just what state the fuse was in. Depending on their type, fuses were immunised by various means. Some might be stopped by a magnetic clock-stopper or have a quick-solidifying agent pumped into it to clog up the mechanism and another could be tackled with a sludge comprising liquid oxygen or nitrogen.

Many fuses also incorporated an anti-handling device, a booby trap, which had to be dealt with. But whatever the means, the fuse had to be disabled before any other work was done on the bomb.

There are two peculiarities of Hermann. Firstly, the explosive filling. Having been so long in the ground, a chemical reaction took place inside that transformed part of the filling to nitro-glycerine, a very unstable and volatile substance. Secondly, a build-up of ammonia within the bomb case. This pressure could increase to about one hundred pounds per square inch. Released suddenly, this would prove lethal in seconds and had done so in the past! So, we went to work.

An electric stethoscope was attached to the bomb case and then it was found that the extension lead for this hadn't been loaded, leaving a few feet between the bomb and whoever was on listening watch, which happened to be me. Being so close to it, I chose to sit on the bomb. The OC used a hammer and chisel on the fuse locking ring. I was horrified. (I was new to the game). I was astride this thing, with headphones on, waiting to hear if the monster would start ticking and all I could hear was the ring of metal on metal. The locking ring came off and then the locating ring and then came the job of removing the fuse, which started ticking!

It then stopped again. The clock-stopper was put in place very quickly. By this time, we were all in a sorry state, drenched and covered in mud and the OC told Mick and myself to go and find a pub and have something to eat. We duly found a pub some way down the road. There were many people in there, mostly those who'd been evacuated from their homes, and they wanted to know when they could go back, and we couldn't tell them!

We were only the junior members of this gang, and it was more than our jobs were worth to predict when the bomb would be made safe or when these people could return to their homes. That was up to the OC and the police respectively. We'd bought this on ourselves though. In the back of the Land Rover were the OC's and Young's combat jackets. Mick and I wore them in the pub. Mick wore Captain Dace's and I wore Lieutenant Young's. They gave us false authority and it was no wonder people asked us for information we couldn't give them. Had we been seen wearing those jackets by their owners, we'd have been in deep shit. We had a pie and a pint and when we got back, the fuse had been extracted, the bomb was made safe and we tidied up, loaded the vehicle and left for Chattenden and I never thought I'd be glad to see that place, but I was that night. Lesson learned. I never stayed behind again, I got away as soon as possible!

The bomb was taken away the next day and disposed of. If it had gone off the night before, the new Tesco supermarket that was scheduled to be built on that site (an old sewage farm) would have been put back some months at least and there wouldn't have been even a tooth filling left of any one of us. The Hermann bomb left a huge crater when detonated.

Recovery of this bomb, however, merited a postage stamp-sized mention in the local paper, which I still have and there were no photographs, but the photo of a typical Hermann gives some idea of its size. Hermann was usually recognised by the 'Kopf' (head) ring, part of which can be seen around the nose.

A recovered Hermann bomb

One November morning I was again on a crash call, and again it was London but this time, the city. Aldersgate had been cordoned off because something looking remarkably like a bomb had been found by GPO workmen while re-laying underground cables. Unfortunately, just around the corner was The Barbican and the Queen Mother was shortly to visit an art club in the GPO building. Traffic had been halted and time was of the essence in the identification and possible removal of the object. Again, it was Captain Dace, Lt. Young and me. The two officers went underground to investigate the suspect metal object while I stayed above ground, with headphones on. Why I was sitting next to the hole I can't recall. I should have been at a safe distance with a field telephone set so I could alert the two officers if I heard any suspect sound from the device but I have to assume that again the extension cable was not included in the crash kit.

At some stage, WO2 Murphy appeared on the scene, followed by a 3-ton truck full of unit members but apart from Murphy, they took no part in the proceedings. I was again on listening watch, waiting for a clock to start up but that wasn't likely to happen as the object was identified as a capped-off water or gas main. The navvies could go on working, traffic started to flow, there were smiles all round and no doubt the Queen Mum could safely look at pictures. We put away the kit and headed back to Chattenden.

There had been photographers around at the time of this incident and one took a photo of me. I was sitting on the ground, headphones on and my beret on the back of my head. I was given the photo a week or so later and told that next time, I should wear my beret in the proper manner. A telling off but only a mild one. It's just as well that our dear sergeant wasn't on that job. I must admit to frequently and wrongly wearing my beret this way. Had I had a decent beret to start with. I probably wouldn't have! Mine was one of those that, worn correctly, made me look like a one-eared spaniel.

Farrow on listening watch
Aldersgate crash call Nov 1966

The next job that came up was a little daunting. A gravedigger/gardener working in the rain at Loughton Jewish Cemetery had seen some purple earth while working and wondering what it was, had pushed it with his foot. He went to the pub after he finished work and took his muddy boots off at the door and left them there. Another regular drinker there, a local bobby asked him where his boots were, and the man explained about the purple mud on his boots.

The copper went to have a look and saw the boots smoking. He'd been around during the war and recognised what he thought might be the filling of an incendiary bomb. This material remains inert until it comes into contact with oxygen. So, it was correctly assumed that an incendiary device had been dropped at the cemetery and had split open. Incendiary bombs are horrendous weapons and cause dreadful burns.

Working in a place like this was always a sensitive issue. There's a question of protocol. What might be acceptable in our own religion may not be in someone else's. George Cooney said that when a hearse went past, we ought to stand to attention and salute. Sgt F maintained that they weren't military funerals, and we need not stand to attention and certainly not salute and I'd back him on this. We'd show our respect by stopping our work and standing up till the cortege had passed us. It's as well that we weren't working in Highgate Cemetery, which was at the bottom of the road where I lived. That was a busy place and had we been there, we'd never have got any work done.

Whereas the ground had been workable when evidence of the bomb was found, it was a different proposition when we went there. The digging started and the ground was as hard as iron. With graves there, the drainage was good and allowed the soil to dry out.

While searching for this bomb, exhumations had to be done and Mick Scott and another sapper contracted severe cases of impetigo from handling corpses and rotten coffins. I never saw the end of this job as I was taken off to attend the Bomb Disposal (BD) course.

All the new boys, and we were classed as such, despite having worked in the unit since January, sat the course. To my mind, this should have taken place on joining the unit. From the beginning of Bomb Disposal, it was policy not to instruct NCO's and sappers in fuse identification. They thought that the lower ranks couldn't be trusted with this knowledge and might take it on themselves to extract fuses to keep as souvenirs. It was also said that ignorance was a grave source of danger and by God, we were ignorant!

We knew the basics of booby-traps but during the course our knowledge was broadened, and we set up many, using pressure, pull and pressure release switches. Anything and everything was rigged up to explode if someone sat on it, leant on it or picked it up. We all set these booby-traps and we all triggered them. Cigarette packets were rigged to explode if picked up and, in the end, no one would dare to lift one. Toilets traps were likewise set for the unwary but these were all IED's and therefore in a different category than the stuff we'd usually see.

We knew never to touch a 'blind' mortar bomb but now we knew why! We set up basic explosive charges and we blew things up (very enjoyable!) and we learnt about things like camouflets. A major danger in bomb disposal work was the hidden menace of the camouflet. This hazard was the result of a bomb exploding underground without making an open crater. A roughly circular, sealed off chamber was formed by the explosion, filled with carbon monoxide gas. It was practice to use a metal probe to follow the bomb's path and if this probe penetrated the chamber, the gas escaped under pressure. One breath of this and it would incapacitate. A little more would kill.

Breaking the crust of a camouflet with a pick or shovel, a man would fall straight through, with no hope of being saved. We may have encountered this while working but had no knowledge of such a danger. This is why I say that we should have been on a course at the outset. I never came across a camouflet and for that, I'm thankful.

We had plenty of lessons in shaft building, which we had some knowledge of, and bomb fuses. Some of that we'd never need as the removal of fuses from bombs was still officer-only territory, but we still had to learn it. A lot of field engineering came into the job, but it was field engineering with a purpose. Unlike combat engineering in a field squadron, we could see an end result from our labours.

Bridge building for the sake of it, over a road or a river, up to my neck in water, never appealed to me. We knew that much of our working life would be spent digging in lousy conditions but if there was a bomb to be found and made safe, it was worthwhile. It was a very interesting course, delivered without condescension and with some humour.

I passed the course, not with any distinction but with a reasonable result. Some didn't pass and although they'd been doing the job for almost a year, a failure meant a posting elsewhere. I can't remember how long the course lasted. It was geared mostly to UK needs.

During 1965, two men from the unit, Major H P Qualtrough MBE and Sergeant H Cooke BEM, were tasked to go to Penang Island, Malaysia. They had the unenviable job of making safe Japanese bombs left behind at the end of the war.

In 1958, the Australian troop of 11 Field Squadron RE, based at Terendak Camp, Malacca, had been tasked with the removal of bombs from sites on Penang and had disposed of many 250kg bombs. These had been in tunnels but over the years, the tunnels had collapsed and the bombs had to be dug out using plant. Unfortunately there was a cave-in one day and two young men, Sappers Bullock and Ryan were buried alive. These men were not bomb disposal trained and the job had been undertaken as a field engineering task.

The job was wrapped up for a time and only reopened after locals had dug up some bombs, emptied them and used the explosive filling for fishing. The Malaysian government of the day then requested assistance in removing the bombs as they had no competent military unit capable of dealing with a task of this magnitude.

Major Qualtrough and Sergeant Cooke examined nine tunnels and trenches, all covered in dense vegetation, which was cleared using local labour. Bombs of up to 500kg were found and disposed of by sea dumping, the recognised method of disposal. Due to lack of manpower and suitable equipment, only part of the job was completed before the two men had to leave for Betio Island, in the Gilbert and Ellis Group, where more munitions were awaiting their attention.

Sgt, H 'Joe' Cooke BEM

At the cessation of hostilities in the Pacific, the Americans had blown up and bulldozed the bunkers there, which had to be excavated by hand. The explosive was again dumped at sea. There were human remains in some bunkers and these had to be re-interred. Both men were awarded well deserved George Medals.

So, after the course finished, we were informed that a team of a dozen or more were required the following year, to carry on in the Far East, where Maj Qualtrough and Sgt Cooke had left off and volunteers were requested. It's axiomatic in the military that no one ever volunteers for anything, but if I hadn't disregarded this piece of 'old sweats' advice, my life would have been shaped quite differently. I'd joined the army as much to travel as anything else and this was an ideal opportunity to do just that.

The successful volunteers would be spending time in Singapore and Malaysia, places that were just names in an atlas to me and wasn't to be missed. I was one of the first to put my name down. Then, all on tender-hooks, we had to wait to see who had been chosen. I was successful but I was more than a little disappointed that Stuart, my best oppo, hadn't been picked. He thinks that Sgt F might have had something to do with this by putting in a bad report about him. Possible!

We were given an extensive brief on what to expect on the other side of the world, the food, the customs, the people and most important of all, what Japanese bombs we were likely to encounter, and the dangers involved in their disposal. Our briefing took in the climate; very different from anything most of us had been used to. They had an average rainfall of one hundred and twenty inches a year.

Not for nothing was their forest called rainforest. Temperatures would vary but would be somewhere in the region of 80 to 90 F and the humidity level was high, meaning we'd sweat a lot.

It was a Muslim nation where we were going. Although this wouldn't affect us, we had to be aware of it. There were three main races there, Malay, Chinese and Indian, all having different customs, different religions, and different food.

One thing from those lectures that stuck in my memory is a description of Chinese cooking, Malaysian style. We were told that most Chinese cooking is done using a wok and that the chef would pour oil into this and heat it up. To test if the oil was hot enough, he'd spit onto it. If the oil was hot enough, the spit would bounce off; if not hot enough, it wouldn't. Think about it! Being just sprogs, we were quite inclined to believe it.

We were briefed on the sex situation and told that VD was rife in both Singapore and Malaysia. The only sure way of avoiding getting 'a dose' was to abstain completely. This was to an audience of lads in their early twenties, so I for one wasn't taking too much notice of this part of the proceedings and from what I saw later, not many of the others heeded it either. You can't keep British squaddies away from the local crumpet, any more than you can keep them away from beer.

Without doubt, we would come across the local wildlife, as we'd be working in secondary jungle and scrub. Some of the wildlife, we were told, would also inhabit whatever camp we happened to be in. Cobras were common, as were pit vipers and as with all snakes, the only thing to do was to give them a wide berth. A snake to be avoided at all costs was the krait, a highly venomous reptile about two feet long, banded in black and white. An interesting snippet of information regarding the krait that had us all sitting up and taking notice was this; if we were bitten by one of these, the best thing to do was to sit quietly and have a cigarette as it would be the last one we'd ever have. Death would be fairly swift. Not a pleasant prospect!

And then we got onto bombs. Many had been removed in 1958, mostly 250kg bombs. More had been removed during 1965 by the Qualtrough/Cooke team but there were still plenty left for us, covering three different weight ratios, 60kg, 250kg and 500kg. A lot of the tunnels and cut and cover trenches had fallen in and been swallowed up by secondary growth and we were warned that in all probability, there could be other munitions buried on the various sites, but there would be no booby-traps.

The terrain was of different types; rubber plantations, marsh and scrubland, not all of it negotiable by vehicle. The lecture covered the dangers of exuded picric acid from leaky bombs, and we must always be aware of this. No steel tools should be used to scrape the earth from them; bronze scrapers had to be used instead. In fact, no steel of any description should come into contact with the bombs. All this information was absorbed, and copious notes were taken.

We lived and ate at 12 RSME Regiment at Chattenden but Lodge Hill Camp was where we trained and where the Joint Services Bomb Disposal School (JSBDS) was located.

We spent most of our working days there. At the beginning, we spent days concreting and road building because the place was only partially built to our needs. It was also where our NAAFI was. At the back, behind the buildings was the training area, a vast expanse of weeds and mud and just before this area was a small shed on the right, heavily padlocked. This had been taken over by the one and only George Cooney and it gradually filled with tools.

Sent to fetch a shovel or other tool from the troops' G1098 store, it was often found that there were none available, so we'd go to Cooney's store. Most of the tools that he had locked away there had, in a previous life, been G1098 or other troops' tools, but George had appropriated them and we had to sign for them, even though he'd pinched them. He'd had much the same arrangement at Broadbridge Heath, where his store had been opposite the guardroom, tucked away behind another building. I'd had no occasion to visit it back then. As explained, George was a real character. I never knew his age, but he'd fought in World War 2 and Korea and maybe some other places. Rumour had it that he wouldn't wear all his medals as this would have given away his age. He said that while in Korea, he was there when the Scotsman from the Black Watch, big Bill Speakman, won his V.C.

Speakman threw grenades at the attacking Chinese and when these ran out, being half drunk, he threw empty beer bottles and anything else he could find. Speakman was awarded a VC, but George was busted down to Lance Corporal for being drunk. No justice there! George had a metal plate inserted into his skull, the result of some wartime wound, and he'd tap it with a metal object and make it ring. He was an entertaining character, full of Irish wit and 'blarney'. He was easy to get on with but had no time for fools.

Argue with him and he'd challenge you to a 'bayonet fight' using broom handles and although bulky and in his sixties, he was incredibly fast and aggressive.

When drunk, he'd march up and down the barrack room, making mouth music to imaginary bagpipes, interspersed with Irish rebel songs but woe betide anyone who even thought of singing a rebel song to him while he was sober. He'd threaten to charge them. 'We're in the Queen's army now,' he'd say.

Cooney had been in the IRA, the proper, uniformed army, not the civvy-clad rabble that we usually associate with that organisation. He joined the British army in Ireland. When asked what his previous job had been, he replied that he'd been a soldier. 'No' said the recruiting sergeant, 'that's what you're about to become.' Cooney insisted he'd been a soldier and the sergeant, probably misunderstanding George's broad Irish brogue, listed him as a solderer.

King's Corporal George Cooney
The best loved character in Bomb Disposal

While at Broadbridge Heath, returning to his billet one winter's night after getting drunk at the Shelley Arms, George slipped and fell and lay in the snow. When he was found, not only did he have cuts and bruises he also had pneumonia and was taken to Horsham Hospital. The RSM,

'Spike' Kelly, took George's documents from the Admin. Office. What he found caused him to destroy some of those documents. George was found to be well over retirement age, which would have been noted at the hospital and George would have been put out to grass and no one wanted that!

Kelly was that sort of RSM, a great man and contrary to the usual way soldier's think of their RSM, we all recognised that he was an exception to the rule. A big man, in all respects, scarred from eye to mouth, a legacy of Korea, he was a sentimental and caring man. I think of him even now as one of the best RSM's to have served in our Corps and there have been some good ones!

The bomb museum had been moved down from Broadbridge Heath and housed in a large building at Lodge Hill. It had to be large, as the collection comprised many very big bombs. There was a Japanese Kamikaze plane, a V1 'Doodle-bug' and the forerunner of today's missiles, a V2 rocket. Whereas many of the bombs at Broadbridge Heath were kept outside, lining both sides of a path between two buildings, most of those at Lodge Hill were kept under cover.

There were a few outside for display purposes, including 'Tallboy' and the biggest of all, Britain's own 'Grand Slam', 10 tons of mischief, a bomb that the Germans couldn't match for size. This was the bomb that put paid to the Tirpitz.

The miscellaneous hardware of war inside the museum was truly awe inspiring. There were bombs of every shape and size, from both Allies and the Axis powers, German, Italian and Japanese and the latter I was going to have a first-hand knowledge of soon. One little beauty there ought to be described. This was the German butterfly bomb. About 4 and a half pounds in weight, it was round bodied, shaped a little like a can, with ends slightly rounded at the edges. They were housed in containers in groups of 23 or 24. Each had a rod sticking out of the top and on this rod was mounted the butterfly vanes or fan. On leaving the aircraft, a charge burst open the container and the bombs fell freely. The spring-loaded vanes opened, the fan went to the top of the rod and locked on. The fan then rotated and armed the device.

Butterfly bombs were often painted bright yellow, presumably to entice children to pick them up. Many did and were killed. Curious cattle and many pets were also killed.

A standard World War Two German butterfly bomb

These bombs were extremely sensitive and when dropped near each other, when one detonated, those in close proximity would also detonate. They can only have been meant as a terror weapon, the first of the three. In my time with Bomb Disposal, I never encountered one of these horrors and I never heard of anyone else finding one either.

These things are still being found but look nothing like they did when dropped. In most cases the spindle and vanes are missing. Looking like a rusty tin can, they will blow up if handled. The last person killed by a butterfly bomb was in 1956. Between 2010 and 2017, nineteen of these devices have been found. They are still as lethal now as they were in 1940.

Where the museum's exhibit came from, I have no idea as I thought it impossible to acquire an unexploded one. They say that imitation is the sincerest form of flattery so these things must have been effective, as the Americans turned them out later by the tens of thousands. At a guess, the museum's exhibit may well have been an American copy.

A Russian MIG jet fighter crashed in a lake or river in West Berlin about this time and the boffins wanted first-hand information of Russian technology. Sgt F was sent off post-haste to Germany to find out what the fighter was carrying in the way of armaments. From reports, he did a good job. While he was away, we departed for Singapore; I never saw him again.

In our NAAFI at Lodge Hill, there were Venetian blinds, and it didn't take long for us to find that the nylon cord used on these made great bootlaces. The blinds were almost stripped of cord. We laced them up tight, so no one knew the cord was gone. It was some time before a staff member dropped the blinds and the whole thing fell apart. We all got a major bollocking over that! My laces lasted a long time.

Coming up to the end of the year, Mr. Kelly, our RSM, was due to retire and a presentation was held at Lodge Hill one night. We'd all chipped in for his going-away gift although I can't remember what was bought. The RSM, big man that he was, wasn't too big that night not to cry. It was moving, seeing tears running down his face. He'd secured a job at Sandhurst Military Academy, but I don't know in what capacity. He died not long after leaving the army. WO1 RSM Woods took over. He was OK but never held our affection as Spike had done.

Another thing that happened was the death of one of our sappers, Billy Neil. It's been reported that he died in March 1967 but we heard about it at the end of 1966, so wires got crossed somewhere. He went out for a boozy night with some mates and apparently went to the JRC at Brompton Barracks and he was found at the bottom of the ravine in front of the club. Whether he was found dead or died later we were never sure. Billy hadn't been in the unit very long, but he was well liked. He was about twenty-three, a ginger-haired Scot and he'd been in the army longer than us. Another young life cut off long before it was due.

We came up to Christmas leave. Scouse Gore came back to London with me and stayed for three days before leaving for Liverpool. We had a lot of drinks together at various pubs. He and my dad sat one night running through the pub names on Liverpool's Scotland Road. I never knew there could be so many bars in one street and apparently, they'd both drunk in all of them, Dad, during the war, while on runs ashore from convoy escort duty and Scouse because it was his manor.

The night before Scouse left, he persuaded me to eat Chinese food. The previous night I'd talked him into eating jellied eels, something he'd in the past rejected as disgusting. He tried them and liked them so much, he had second helpings! With this in mind, I could hardly refuse to eat Chinese food with him.

We got a taxi to an upmarket restaurant called the Bamboo House, somewhere Up West and we went in uniform. I'd early found that it was usually good for a couple of pints. I sat next to a woman at the bar who commented on our uniform and asked what the bomb badge on the sleeve was for. We told her it was the Bomb Disposal unit badge. She asked us about our job, and we told her a little of the tasks we'd been on. She was enthralled. She introduced herself as Sheila Scott and she said she was a small-plane pilot. It then clicked that she was Britain's own aviatrix. No free drinks that night though.

Anyway, I was inducted into eating Chinese food and quite enjoyed it, not an inappropriate transition considering where we were going the following year. I was saddened to learn much later that Sheila Scott, despite being an author and a flyer of some note, ended her days living in a bedsit, dying in poverty. England didn't look after its flying heroine.

I spent Christmas at my brother's home and the family all came there on Christmas Day for lunch. Who knew when or if we'd meet again? Not I! Men had died while working on the Penang job so a lot of time was spent boozing with my brother as I had no idea of what awaited me or even if I'd return home again.

My brother and sister-in-law came to the station with me when it was time to go and it was with a lump in my throat that I said goodbye.

The trip down to Strood wasn't exactly a happy one but at that age there isn't really time to be depressed so the dark mood quickly evaporated. Back to Chattenden I went and back into normal work, but we had no tasks to do outside. I'm not saying there were none, just that those of us being sent overseas didn't go out on any jobs.

We queued up for the necessary inoculations, some of which made us ill. The yellow fever shot was a swine, as was the TABT! After having these shots, it was normal army procedure to have us working out in the gym, to get it circulating and people did collapse from this. It's since been recognised that the best practice is for those inoculated to rest, but we're talking about the 1960's army. Very little changes over time with the British military and it would have taken years for this to be accepted and used.

We had to be kitted out with jungle green uniform, known as OG'S (olive green!) Everything, from towels to washing case was olive drab and the underpants likewise and they were huge! These were known by us as 'drawers Drac', Drac being short for Dracula, but I don't know the connection. Even he wouldn't wear stuff like this and none of us ever did! I'm sure there was some sort of logic in making it possible for air to circulate in our nether regions, but I'm equally sure that a better model could have been made.

The best part of this new kit was the cotton pyjamas, the only article of clothing that wasn't green. Pale blue, in fact. Although few of us ever wore them out east, I did wear them in 'civvy street' and they lasted well into the 90's. There were various other items of kit needed for serving in a hot, wet environment. The webbing was 44 pattern jungle kit, used during the last war but eminently suitable for use in the sixties. We'd been issued with a standard army pattern machete, known to the troops as a 'tree beater'. The back of the blade would have served as a hammer, or one could possibly floor an opponent with it but the blade was useless for cutting. It wasn't hollow ground and wouldn't hold an edge, hence the name tree beater. But it was issue kit and along with a first aid dressing, our water bottle and jack knife, it constituted our belt kit.

Infantry soldiers would laugh at the paucity of our belt kit, considering that the communist threat still existed. The RE jack knife was another fairly useless tool; alright for opening cans but being stainless steel, also wouldn't hold an edge and later, on site out east, I carried a flick knife that did! I still have a standard jack knife and a tree beater, dated 1966, with ↑, the broad arrow of the MoD. We'd have been better off if we'd been issued kukris. Our No 2 dress uniforms were going with us but wrapped and packed. And a first for me was getting photographed for a passport, something I'd never needed before. I was looking forward to getting away from dull, cold 'Blighty' to somewhere where the sun was shining. I was at the age where I could enjoy the upcoming adventure.

PART TWO

'SINGERS'

Chapter Nine

We got through airport formalities and bundled ourselves and our luggage into a 3-ton truck that was waiting for us outside. By the time we got to Gillman Barracks it was about 0100. We were dropped off at the guardroom where we were each given a packet of sandwiches. How long they'd been there I have no idea, but they were crawling with tiny black ants. Most of us wouldn't touch these curly-edged sandwiches with their strange filling but Mick Rose and Tim Vismer fell on them with delight. Mick told us they were sugar ants and were very good. I took his word for it as he stuffed his mouth. I must explain that Tim had been born and brought up in Rhodesia and Mick in Kenya, where eating insects is obviously commonplace, even for whites! It wasn't to be the only time I saw them do this.

We had been billeted in 59 Field Squadron block and bedding had been laid out for us, complete with mosquito net. It was the first time I'd seen this arrangement. Malaria had been eradicated in Singapore, but no malaria didn't mean no mosquitoes. Given half a chance they'd have eaten us alive that night. We were worn out.

Flying isn't the relaxing past-time that travel brochures would have us believe and unless you're in business or first class, being comfortable is difficult. There's never enough leg room and trying to sleep sitting up eventually hurts the neck. So, after all those hours in the air, I fell asleep easily.

The next morning saw us trying to orientate ourselves to a completely different lifestyle. We all made it to breakfast, and it was the usual army meal, renowned wherever the British Army takes up residence, rubber eggs, greasy bacon and greasy beans. How did they manage to make baked beans run with fat like that?

Being so new to the climate, I couldn't eat hot food in the middle of the day, so I opted for salad for lunch and the salads were good. The only problem with that was I was still hungry and going for a second helping was a non-starter. I filled the gap by eating what was left of Gordon Whipp's salad. I brought the lunchtime talk round to what types of dirty hands or foul insect had been on the food and had the cooks washed it properly. Poor old Gordon had a bit of a weak stomach and after a few sentences, he'd push his plate away. I pulled it over and got a filthy look as a reply to my question of whether he wanted his food or not. This way I got extra rations.

We paraded later and went to EBI, the Engineer Base Installation, where we were to spend many days; days of getting the necessary equipment together, days of testing and re-testing. Once up country, if there was any sort of shortage or breakdown, we'd be left high and dry. We had to acclimatise, and this meant wearing shirts while out in the sun. Failure to do so would have meant being badly burnt. Working outside was very wearing to those of us who'd only known England's watery sun. Temperatures of 90F were unknown to most of us and few had had experience of high humidity, so being drenched in sweat after ten minutes took some getting used to.

During this time, I found that our OC had a mania for badges and insignia. Along with our jungle kit, we'd been issued with the customary miner's helmet but this time, in white. I was given the task of painting badges on the front of each helmet, on the clip where a light would normally sit.

My past exploits with a pencil and paper had somehow got to the ears of higher authority. I didn't mind this job at all and while the other team members shifted kit, I got down to painting ducky little bombs on each helmet. It was something easily handled, and it did give me some indication of what to expect in the future.

The sights and sounds of a tropical garrison were so different that it was sometimes hard to take it all in. Walking to the cookhouse for lunch one day, I saw a big lizard on a tree trunk, a few feet from the ground. I caught it with one hand while distracting it with the other. It was that easy! It was some sort of iguana, about two feet long. I was told to take care or the thing would bite me. I knew it wouldn't. I'd kept a much bigger lizard than this as a teenager, but the average Brit thinks that anything unknown is dangerous.

The house geckos, much smaller cousins of the iguana, fascinated me, pink, translucent creatures that could walk on walls or upside down on ceilings with ease. They sometimes laid their two eggs in our lockers and when getting an article of kit out, having one run up one's arm came as a shock. They were totally harmless little things and even today, remain one of my favourites.

Other local wildlife that occasionally made its home in our lockers wasn't so welcome. These were large spiders. Some had bodies two inches long and quite large fangs and although I had no problems with lizards of any size, I didn't trust these beasts at all.

One thing I thought strange at first was the total lack of twilight. It was light and then it was dark, no lingering daylight until eight or nine at night that we'd get in England; just a ten-minute lessening of light, the sun went down and it was then night.

Since those days I've spent nearly twenty-five years in the tropics, but I still miss the summer light, hanging on in the sky. Mornings were the same, dark at 07:00 and light about fifteen minutes later.

Wednesday afternoon in the British Army is called 'reccy' afternoon. The idea originally had been to use it for sports and although some did, most spent the time in town or at the pool or just loafing around the barrack room. They had a good pool at Gillman but, at that time, I was a non-swimmer, so it didn't get a lot of use from me. We weren't there long enough to get really settled in and no doubt there would be a pool in the next camp where I could learn.

During the first evening, we were introduced to an institution well-known to British soldiers from the eastern Mediterranean to Hong Kong, the charwallah. He might be called either chywallah or charwallah, but he fulfilled the same function; providing glasses of hot, sweet tea or orange juice and fried egg sandwiches, known as egg banjos. Gillman Barracks charwallahs were all Pakistani Muslims, so no bacon sarnies. Although the charwallah ran a book, we didn't qualify as we weren't permanent, and we had to pay each time we ordered. Every squadron had their own charwallah, who ran his little empire from the end room on the bottom floor of each barrack block.

On one occasion while we were there, the 54 Sqn. charwallah had upset someone and when he came in one morning, he found the breakfast bacon wrapped round the door handle of his room. He just turned round and walked off. He lost a day's takings, but the lads lost too. No egg banjos or tea that day and there were other repercussions, as the squadron was paraded and told to cease with actions like this.

Another necessary fixture in the garrison was the boot-boy. As the name implies, he cleaned our boots and our belt brasses and brass shoulder titles. This cost two Singapore dollars per man, per week but even with that low cost, there were always some who tried to dodge paying.

Another indispensable member of the community was the dhobi wallah, who'd have your kit, civvy and military, washed and ironed and back by the next day, shirts starched and so crisp that they would stand up on their own and all this for a paltry few dollars each week.

Once a week an old Chinese lady would potter around the blocks: this was Sew-Sew and she would sit in a corner and put on shoulder flashes, sew on buttons, and do general repairs and for very little. After having to do all this

Jonesy, the boot-boy

ourselves back in England, I found these amenities well worth the money.

We generally went out in a gang during the day, Gordon Whipp, Mick Rose, Jim Stow, Les Wardle, Tim Vismer, Scouse Gore, John Green, Bob Nesbitt and me. John Green, being married, chaperoned us, and wouldn't have come out with us had we been after crumpet. Les was also married but I never knew this.

One afternoon we went into a bar and saw a crowd of RE sergeants at a table, one of whom was our own Sgt 'Joe' Cooke, the man who'd done the recce for our upcoming job. We introduced ourselves and had a chat with him, but I couldn't help feeling he was taken aback at our youthful appearance. There was 'Joe', somewhere around the 40-year-old mark, a be-medalled veteran of the last war, holder of the BEM and later, the GM, talking to a load of kids young enough to be his sons, kids who were going to take over where he left off.

We had a lot to live up to and I hope that when he read the reports, as I'm sure he would have done, he wasn't dissatisfied with the results of the job or with our conduct.

A lot of our free time in Singapore was spent sight-seeing and we went to various places, including Haw Par Villa and other tourist traps. It was all good fun. I'd read about Singapore in books at home and knew about the 'Dirty Half Mile' of pre-war fame although no one could tell me where it was.

The city was full of bars, and we drank in most of them. We walked when most people went by taxi. It was the only way to see the place properly and it was during one of these walks near Keppel Harbour one afternoon that we came across street hawkers, cooking food by the roadside.

We didn't eat anything, but one smell has remained with me from that encounter; the smell of food frying in coconut oil. It is distinctive and can't be mistaken for anything else. I've smelt it recently and the memories came flooding back and I was twenty-two again! Smells are far more evocative than sights or sounds.

Our sojourn in Singapore came to an end on the 9th March, when two 3-ton trucks turned up to take us north. We loaded one truck with the equipment we'd need to do the job and we boarded the other one. Two lance corporals from the Royal Corps of Transport were our drivers. These were Dave Woolmer and Jim Land, great blokes. They were from 28 Commonwealth Brigade, based in Malaysia, at Terendak Camp, Malacca and they were part of 3 Squadron RCT, a unit we were destined to have much to do with in the future.

Chapter Ten

OPERATION BOMBS PENANG

After Singapore, I found Malaysia very boring. While travelling, there were mile after mile of rubber trees. At least, this is the impression I got from the back of a truck. Today, the rubber has gone and it's mile after mile of oil palm but still as boring as hell.

The only break in this regimented green panorama was the occasional small village, known as a kampong, with small houses on stilts. The women would be bathing, fully clothed, in the rivers beside the road.

The route we took, no highways having then been invented, was Johor Bahru, Yong Peng, Segamat, Tampin and then Seremban, where we were to spend the night. I jotted down some place names from road signs I'd seen so I could tell my brother about the trip. Somewhere on this road, while stopping for a pee, Dave Woolmer went into a field and came back with a huge watermelon, which he chopped up with his golok (machete). He shared it out between us.

We didn't stop for food on the way as we'd been issued with the army's answer to starvation, the infamous 'packed lunch'. It was dark when we pulled into Seremban

Camp, and we had a meal prepared by the duty cook. It's a fair assumption to say that every duty cook in the army resents having to cater for late comers, no matter what the reason is for them not being on time and this one was no exception.

The food is generally left-overs from the garrison's evening meal, thrown together quickly so the cook can get back to the bar or whatever he was doing before. This camp was totally different from the Singapore garrison in that the cookhouse was an open air one. There was a roof and a half wall up to about three feet from the ground.

All I can recall about the place is a huge area, lit by fluorescent tubes, which give any place at night a lonely, desolate look! The barrack blocks weren't as high as those down south either.

Next morning, those of us who had the stomach for it, had breakfast and I wasn't one of them. We piled onto the truck and set out north again. The route we took that day is less clear but one place I can remember is Petaling Jaya, then a small township tacked on the edge of Kuala Lumpur and now a huge metropolis in its own right and therefore totally charmless. I recall passing a school with Petaling Jaya on its front.

From there we went to Ipoh, bypassed Taiping, went through Nibong Tebal and then headed for Butterworth, which was as far as we were going on the mainland. (Dave Woolmer confirmed that this is the route we took after leaving Seremban.) Due to the lack of bridges on our route, when there was a river across our path, it had to be negotiated by ferry; flat barges just big enough to carry a truck. We had to endure two or three of these on our trip north. The next expanse of water we encountered was the channel between the mainland and Penang Island. Bigger ferries this time, big enough to take our 3-tonners and a host of other trucks, cars, motorbikes, pushbikes and what seemed like hundreds of people. I was to become well acquainted with the Penang ferries as time went on. It had been a long, dusty and fairly uncomfortable trip, as 3-tonners aren't fitted out with passengers in mind.

After leaving the ferry, the drive to Minden Barracks was fairly short. The camp was situated along the eastern edge of the island, in sight of the sea. Like all far eastern barracks, it was built just before the last war, in time for the Japanese to take them over and turn them into places of horror. We were part of Penang Garrison and yet, not a part in the accepted sense of the word. We shared their camp but were administered independently.

The 2nd Battalion Royal Green Jackets was the resident infantry battalion and with them we ate but nothing more. I liked this camp from the outset. It was very hilly, with plenty of greenery; bamboo and shrubs everywhere and plenty of wide open spaces. We were given a set of rooms to ourselves at the top end of the camp, rooms airy, clean and light and in these we quickly set up home. The bed spaces had been allocated to us and I was in a room with Lance corporal Jim Land, Sappers Gordon Whipp and Mick Rose.

We had access to the 2 RGJ's NAAFI and the cookhouse, also any sports facilities, like the swimming pool and we were bound by their disciplinary procedures for leaving camp. As with all barracks abroad, we had to book out and book back in.

Our first day in this new location was given over to sorting out the kit we'd brought with us and housing it in its new home, which was a woefully inadequate small building at the bottom of a slope leading to the lower end of camp.

It was in a well shaded spot however, so we could dispense with jackets while working. The mosquitoes must have thought it was Christmas! We were unmistakably new boys, all white, with brand new uniforms. It was to be a while before we all 'got our knees brown'. I can't account now for the 'bolshie' attitude we had at that time. That we had one is plain because I have a photo of the team, minus Taff, who took the photo, with a red flag held out between us. Being soldiers, we were naïve if we expected anything different in this new location other than what we'd been used to back in England, but we obviously did.

Our OC was plant man. He knew much about earth moving machinery and had in fact been the OC of a RE Plant Squadron and therefore must have been well qualified to command men. Where then was our ill feeling directed and why? This attitude continued for some time, over two months if I recall correctly. Maybe it was that we, as a team, were dissatisfied with being treated like kids and wanted to do the job we'd been sent out for, not forever cleaning rooms.

The OC, Maj. A J Loch

After about two weeks, we were instructed to hand in one OG shirt each and these were taken to the regimental tailor. Although the winged-shield shoulder flash of FARELF was retained on the right sleeve, because we were only on detachment, the Singapore RE Garrison shield was removed from the left. In its place was sewn the legendary, arch-backed black cat of the immortal 17th Indian Division. As we were officially now British Forces North Malaya, we wore this Div sign.

This division, led by 'Punch' Cowan was part of 14th Army and was instrumental in thrashing Jap in the war in Burma and was known in the Indian Army as 'God Almighty's Own'. We really were moving in exalted spheres. I am as proud of this emblem as I was of our own bomb badge. The second shirt followed within days and we were properly kitted-out. These shirts were kept for best and once established, we wore for work any shirt that came to hand. There were always plenty of old shirts to be had at the tailors and we all ended up with at least half a dozen each.

The first site we went to was at Sungai Nibong, which was down the road in the direction of the airport, and it was a great day for us. We'd at last started the job. This was basically our breaking in period, where we learnt just what we had to do over the course of the next year. We had to get our hands hardened up. Too long had been spent doing no digging or hard work. The bomb locators were put to good use here, after suitable holes had been drilled.

We used Australian Proline augers, good pieces of equipment. In decent soil they'd bore a hole four inches in diameter up to fifty feet deep. But we didn't have good soil, we had clay, rock and laterite and we had problems. We could manage two, thirty-five feet deep holes per day, on a good day! On a bad day we'd be using four-inch hand augers and it was slow work. Blisters aplenty! When a hole had been bored to depth, the bomb locator was lowered down the hole and readings taken and plotted on a graph.

Along with difficult digging conditions, our main worries were mosquitoes and leeches. We had no physical protection against 'mossies' they were too small and too fast, but we took Paludrine tablets daily to try to keep malaria at bay. Leeches were a different matter. They'd drop from the trees onto us, and it became a normal procedure for us to watch overhead when we could and only sit on bare earth and at intervals, drop our trousers and inspect.

After acclimatisation we worked without shirts so each could see if a leech was at work on a mate. Wearing jungle boots helped keep them from getting up the trouser legs. Other denizens of the undergrowth were not really a problem to us, although one I certainly didn't like. This was the Golden Orb Spider, which sat in the middle of a huge web, normally strung between two trees. They were venomous and I kept away from them.

There were many streams to be crossed while we were moving about the scrub. Negotiating one of these in the Land Rover on a broken down, rickety bridge, the wheels broke through. New shoring was needed and when this was forthcoming, it was good old Les Wardle who insisted that he was the one to get into the water and work. No one else wanted to get in there and for good reason, leeches! Les wasn't deterred and came out covered in the things. Some of these leeches were very large. Leeches are more of a nuisance than danger but some people could react allergically to them and enough of them could take a fair amount of blood.

There were huge scorpions, at least six inches long, the Malaysian Black Scorpions, living in holes in the ground. We occasionally came across one while clearing the ground for digging. It was a fairly aggressive species and venomous like all scorpions but OK as long as it was left alone. The Atlas Hawk Moths would delight any student of Lepidoptera. They were really large moths, the females having a wingspan of over nine inches.

Water monitors were in abundance, from brightly coloured youngsters eighteen inches long to grandfathers.

This monitor can grow to ten feet in length. Again, not a problem as they quickly made themselves scarce. We might have encountered snakes while pushing through the scrub, but we didn't often see them and avoided any we came into contact with. A snake will get out of harm's way if it can and avoids confrontation where possible. I saw only one instance of a snake being approached too closely and it was a deliberate attempt to annoy the reptile.

We had in the team one individual who knew it all or thought he did. He was a tall, skinny, sullen streak and arrogant with it. He was teasing a small snake, a snake with green and yellow bands, bright red under the tail. I was a keen amateur herpetologist, and I knew what this reptile was, and I was waiting for it to bite him. It was a young Green Pit Viper and quite capable of making him seriously ill. He would have got no help from me. He didn't like me, and the feeling was entirely mutual. Why we didn't get on I don't know but it was one of those cases where individuals instantly take a dislike to each other. We had had a couple of verbal run-ins already and generally avoided each other.

We'd been told on our briefing back at the JSBDS to avoid the wildlife if possible and here was this fool, goading a venomous snake. As it turned out, he then left it alone, avoiding hospital time. I haven't named him due to the laws of libel but if he or any other surviving member of the team ever reads this, they'll know who I refer to.

On our frequent trips through Sungai Nibong, we'd noticed posters being put up on the coffee shop walls and on checking, we saw that a show was advertised, running

Me with pit vipers, under supervision!
Snake Temple

for one week. What type of show, we knew not but whatever it was it would get us out of camp, and we could at least have a beer in different surroundings. I think there were four or five of us who went there one night. We got a beer each and settled down in the row of chairs facing a very home-made stage. The chairs quickly filled up and we got some very strange looks from the locals, all Chinese and all males. This should have told us something, but it failed to register.

A Chinese girl came on. (The performers were all Chinese). We went there expecting something along the lines of a Chinese opera or similar show, but it was far removed from that. No cultural show this, but a sex show, the likes of which we'd never imagined. The girl did a conventional strip to riotous applause from the locals in the front rows of seats. I'd never seen a strip show and most of those with me hadn't either. We'd deliberately kept to the rear seats so we could extricate ourselves easier if there was any bother, but we now realised that we couldn't see much because what was happening on stage was being blocked by the heaving mass of humanity at the front.

This got worse when the second act came on. A bed was wheeled on, complete with a female. She went into her solo act with an empty beer bottle. The crowd at the front, baying like a pack of dogs, were almost standing on each other's shoulders, and trying to get on stage and had to be restrained by a couple of bouncers.

A few more acts followed, a male/female simulated act and a couple more strip acts like the first and then the show was over. This was 1967 and what we'd just seen was unbelievable. When we got back to camp, we went to the NAAFI and told the rest of them what we'd just witnessed. Some of them went the next night but it was a standard Chinese opera being shown and they came back very disgruntled and accused us of inventing the whole story. I ended up half believing I'd imagined it all. I suppose had we all been God-fearing little boys we'd have turned our backs on this show and left but we weren't, we were squaddies, so we stayed and watched.

Just to liven things up for us, a couple of dogs were brought in that could presumably save us a lot of work by sniffing out explosives. One of these dogs was named Panda and I still have the newspaper cutting about its uncanny ability in detecting mines and bombs. It must have been having an off day when it was with us as I can't recall the animal actually finding anything! And even dousing was tried at one stage.

The Japanese had used Penang as a naval base and the harbour housed submarines and motor torpedo boats, while the small airport was used by the naval air force. They didn't have their munitions close by, but had them secreted in the foothills near the main Bayan Lepas-Georgetown road which runs along the east coast of the island. They had workshop facilities at some locations also and all in trenches and tunnels, all built using slave labour. Over the passage of time, these complexes had fallen in and been swallowed up by secondary jungle. The islanders had got used to having bombs on their doorsteps and were quite resigned to it and most had almost forgotten about them.

It was in 1956 that official memories were jolted into reawakening when over 150 bomb cases appeared on the Penang scrap market. This prompted the Malayan government of the time to do something positive. Action was taken on a couple of occasions after this, but no concerted effort was made by a bomb disposal unit to remove the ordnance. Before this, the Emergency had been the top priority and eliminating the Communist threat was paramount.

During May the 'A' Class World War Two Submarine HMS Anchorite berthed in Penang Roads and somehow down the grapevine came an invitation to those who were interested to go aboard and look round. Always ready for something different, I put my name down and about eight of us were ferried to the docks and taken out to the sub.

I took some photos approaching the boat but understandably, none were allowed to be taken onboard for security reasons. The Officer of the Watch entertained us and showed us round what I thought was a very confined work and living space.

Obviously, the torpedoes had more of our interest than anything else, but I was also interested in the deck gun. It was strange to think that this old tub had no doubt been in action before most of us were born. We spent about half an hour there and I remarked to Gordon Whipp that it must have been hell in one of these things in action and weren't we lucky to be able to do our job with plenty of room to move about.

It's been said that submariners must be a special breed of men, different from the usual run of RN ratings, as it was an environment where everyone had to get along and I could think of one team member who I wouldn't want to be cooped up with for months on end in one of these things.

We'd been treated very hospitably on the sub and in return, the crew were invited to our bar. A couple of days later, they turned up in force and a boozy, rowdy night was had by all. We enjoyed their company and they got a good run ashore.

This was our first brush with the navy while in the east but there was a second not long after. I can't remember what ship we visited. I'm sure it was a small one so it was probably a frigate. All I can recall is, on leaving, with RN officers lined up at the brow, we all saluted and instead of saluting army style, I saluted RN fashion, palm-down, which got a big grin from one of the officers. Why I did it, I have no idea and I'm glad it was taken in good part.

HMS Anchorite May 1967
I'm dropping these photos in to prove these events
happened and that I'm not making this up as I go along

Work on the first four tunnels was difficult due to the amount of rock present so we dug away the earth from one tunnel mouth and a 60kg bomb was discovered. (All bombs located and removed will be classed in metric weight). This bomb proved to be something of an embarrassment because we had no means of getting rid of it and it had to be re-interred. Some light gauge railway lines were discovered in another tunnel, some unidentified objects, (which remained unidentified!) and practice depth charges. These also had to be left as there was no way of knowing if they were safe to handle, there being no safety mechanism incorporated in them.

Another driver had been sent to us from Terendak Camp as OC's driver. This was Brian Shuker. He was billeted in our room and a move-round of beds quickly made space for him. He was to keep me laughing for the short time he was with us. Like the rest of us, he got thoroughly fed up with the continuing bullshit and as a mark of his disapproval, he asked me to paint a hammer and sickle on his chest, which I did. He then went around saying 'Kosygin forever!' He was recalled when 3 Squadron RCT wanted him back for a swimming gala and another driver, who I think was Brian Ridley, took his place.

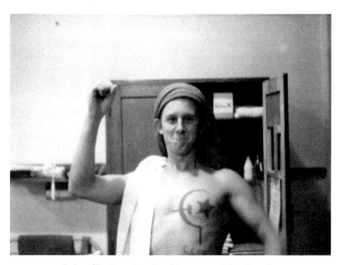

Brian Shuker showing his support for Russia.
May 1967

This spate of bullshit had kicked off two months earlier and was still ongoing. I can only assume that at some stage our sergeant had taken it into his head to inspect the rooms, looking for things to complain about, as sergeants are apt to do.

Equally, it could have been our OC or indeed, an officer of 2 RGJ. This prompted a rash of orders to the effect that room NCOs were to ensure that rooms were swept and kept neat and tidy at all times. In reply to this I made out a list of names of those in our room. Top of this list was Lance corporal Jim Land, who told me to take his name off. (I'd put it on without asking him and he was no doubt thinking of his standing as a junior NCO). No problem, his name was removed and the rest of us had our names printed out thus:

MCTC PENANG GARRISON

Inmates

Sappers Farrow R.

Rose M. Whipp G.

Dvr Shuker B. RCT

On room inspection, I was bollocked by the sergeant for having the audacity to put this notice up and we got the usual stuff about 'We don't know how lucky we are' and 'we don't know when we're well off' and 'it could all be much worse' etc. etc. and I was ordered to take it down immediately.

A second sergeant was drafted in from HQ Bomb Disposal; Vernon 'Chippy' Woods was another Scouse and proved to be totally different from George Duncan. He was still a sergeant with all a sergeant's ideas on what made things tick but he was easier to get on with. George was a new sergeant and was a little unsure of himself and this made him a bit stuffy at times.

Sgt Vernon 'Chippy' Woods

At this time, plant started to arrive from 54 FARELF Support Squadron in Singapore. The first item on site was a Bray light-wheeled tractor.

Now we had plant and vehicles with us, the OC got it into his head that all of them had to be identified by a bomb badge so once again I had to get out my brushes and paint the unit sign on each vehicle. The two 3-ton trucks were left severely alone as they already had 28 Brigade signs painted on them and the OC had no authority to interfere with their markings. The OC also decreed that he wanted miniature plates painted, depicting all the sleeve badges associated with our task and I painted eight of those, which hung on the wall outside his office. None of this I minded in the least.

4073 LCT Ardennes
Arriving to offload plant

While I was painting badges, I wasn't involved in the silly cleaning jobs always found when work was slack.

This month of June found eight of us having a monumental booze- fuelled Saturday afternoon in the NAAFI, on the occasion of the 21ˢᵗ birthday of Danny Watts, a 2 RGJ rifleman and he had three of his mates with him, Chris Young, Pete Watson and another known only as 'Whacker', another Scouse. Danny invited four of us and we ended up with fifty pints of draught Tiger beer in front of us and it was hard work getting through my quota. I got gloriously drunk that afternoon, was found asleep in the toilet and never touched a drop of beer for at least three days.

Although the grubbing up of 60kg bombs by the locals had been going on for years, it was spasmodic. However, with us being around the news must have circulated that this wonderful source of illicit free explosive was about to be taken far beyond reach of their grubby, thieving fingers. Their efforts to dig up bombs accelerated and on the 11th of June an explosion took place near Bukit Gedong. On investigation, it was thought that the locals had removed about one hundred, 60kg bombs. What caused the explosion and who may have been injured we never knew and never cared. They shouldn't have been playing with this stuff to start with.

The police were called in and they searched and found twenty-four cases, with most of the explosives removed, all of it destined for illegal fishing. Six half-filled bombs were found and left behind under police guard. The remainder of the cases were taken back to camp and what explosive they contained was burnt. We'd been working on the island without any real decision having been taken by the Malaysian government on whether we would do this job or not, but this incident galvanised them into action.

The decision to start full-time operations was soon taken and an agreement was signed to this effect and we started on 15th June. The quicker we managed to move the bombs from the site, the better it would be. The RAF Marine Craft Unit disposed of the six half-filled bombs by sea dumping.

An event then took place that changed all our lives; 2nd RGJ left Penang; their tour of duty finished. We'd obviously been expecting this, but it impacted us more than we first realised. For one thing, we had to leave our superb accommodation and find somewhere else to sleep and we could no longer use the Junior Ranks Club, the NAAFI. Another major change was our eating arrangements and the reason behind this was the incoming infantry battalion. It was 2nd Battalion /10th Princess Mary's Own Gurkha Rifles, to give them their full title. The Gurkha's subsisted on a diet of goat curry and rice and while we weren't averse to the occasional curry downtown after a night on the beer, we wouldn't want to eat it every day. There were also cultural differences.

The Gurkhas were great blokes, but we weren't allowed to mix with them. At this time, in the battalion was the only serving VC. He was then a sergeant, and his name was Rambahadur Limbu. (I was outside Buckingham Palace the day of his investiture).

It was decreed at high level that we had to move out and find different recreation and messing areas and alternative sleeping arrangements.

Chapter Eleven

When 2 RGJ left, we suddenly found that apart from the odd Australian over from Butterworth, we were the only white's around, and this gave us a certain novelty value with the girls in town. A few Indians used the bars, but it was mainly Chinese who drank there so we had little competition for most of the time. Each of us had our own personal and very friendly girls in the bars we used and I suppose it was every soldiers dream. And then the Yanks came!

The war in Vietnam was at its height and American servicemen came to Penang on R&R, and from being No1's, we were relegated to way down the list while they were in town. It was inevitable, as they came in with bigger rolls of money than we or the girls had ever seen, and they threw it around.

I saw a GI buy an ivory ornament from a roadside stall and when he asked the price and was told how much it cost, he paid in US dollars! The storekeeper must have thought it was his birthday. He'd meant Malay dollars so the rate of exchange meant he could shut up shop for the rest of the week. Fighting soldiers, they may have been but they were terribly naïve, as the following incident shows.

We decided to go to town to see just how these people operated. We scratched together the taxi fare and enough for one beer each, knowing that if the worst came to the worst, we could always walk back. There were five of us, so we didn't worry about our safety. We asked the cab driver where the Yanks hung out and he took us to the Mandarin Hotel, a favourite GI hang-out. We went to the bar and ordered beers.

An American sitting at the bar leaned over and asked us where we came from. He'd heard our accents and probably couldn't make us out. We told him we came from 'up the road a bit'. We knew what he meant but were being awkward. He said he didn't mean that, he meant what country were we from. We told him we came from England, at which he leaned over and shouted to his mates that we were Limeys. We told him we were not Limeys, we were English. He then said that they called all English Limeys. Gordon asked him what he preferred being called, a Yank or an American. Oh, an American every time he said. Well, we prefer to be called English. He finally got it!

He asked us what we did and we told him. We didn't need to ask him what job he did, we knew. By the time we got on friendly terms with this bloke, it was well past midnight. He'd been buying the beers. We told him a load of rubbish about only being allowed out of camp once a month, being generally badly treated and never having enough money, as our wages were low and compared to his they were! After hearing this, he was buying beers all round.

He gave Gordon a $50 note and asked him to 'set 'em up' while he went to play some pool. Gordon waved this in front of us and we were out of the door and calling for trishaws in the next breath. I can't remember where we went after that, but it was a long way from the Mandarin. I said the Americans were naïve because no British soldier would have entrusted a stranger with his money while he was out of sight of it, and I doubt if any one of us would have believed the fairy story we told him.

I could never understand why he never came to the camp to chase us up but maybe he was too drunk to remember what we told him. A low trick of ours, you might think and maybe it was but at least no one got hurt. Our predecessors in the east, the Royal Marines and The Cameronians used to waylay American Air Force officers, beat them up and take their wallets.

The locating of bombs was temporarily suspended while we moved house. We ended up in the furthest reaches of the camp and as there were no proper brick-built buildings around, living in attap bashas. These at first were looked down on and generally ridiculed but this is all we had, and this is what we had to use. We got used to them. With lighting and big ceiling fans, they were airy enough and having only wooden shutters and no windows, air could circulate.

The walls ended six inches from the ground, allowing more air and unfortunately, other less welcome things to get in. We took over six rooms as sleeping accommodation, four men to each room and we also had stores and offices. We more than once said that the Gurkha's should have had our bashas and we should have been billeted in their homes.

I have nothing but admiration and respect for the Gurkha soldier. He leads the field in bravery and devotion to duty. The potential Gurkha soldier would walk anything up to ten days to get to the recruiting depot and he'd do it barefoot. He'd take no luggage because what he owned was minimal. When he reached his destination, he'd be tested physically and mentally and if he was successful, he'd be recruited into the Brigade. There were always more applicants than places to receive them. The Gurkha recruit would be issued with bedding. Although many preferred to sleep on the floor, they would in time have to use the mattress and blankets. They'd be issued with boots and new boots to feet that have never worn them are a refined form of torture but they would persevere because they had to. They successfully changed their whole lifestyles. They adapted! The Gurkha soldier was tidy and as smart as paint but many of their women had a totally different outlook on life. Gurkha barrack rooms were inspected by British Officers and had to be in tip-top condition, but the Gurkha married quarters were a different proposition entirely.

Whatever the social or military standing of a British army wife, she knows how to, and will, use a gas or electric cooker. Not so the Gurkha wives! Despite being shown the benefits of these appliances and being instructed in their use, these women resolutely refused to use them and rolled back the carpets in the living room and built fires in the middle of the floor. In some cases, they didn't even remove the carpet and just hacked a square from it. A few bricks to hold the pot and that was their cooking area. It was a huge headache for the PWD and QM's departments. All this damage had to be repaired and paid for, but no amount of censure could get them to change their ways. This problem only came to light when the carpet in one quarter caught fire and the blaze quickly spread. This is why we said the accommodation should be swapped over, with us in the married quarters and the married Gurkha families in our bashas. They would have had no carpets to contend with.

A new face arrived on the scene. This was LCpl Bob Grey who'd been seconded to us from 59 Field Squadron as the Admin Cpl or as the Corps knows it, the Orderly Cpl. Now, I can understand a full squadron of upwards of one hundred and fifty personnel having someone to fill this slot, as I'd done the job myself but I failed to see why we needed one as there were only about twenty of us.

However, whatever the reason for Bob being there, he did a good job. Apart from his grasp of administrative duties, he was a qualified electrician, not a bad carpenter, could drive and also ride a motorbike, one of which the OC had purchased from an officer who'd left the island. Bob also helped out on the sites when not involved in office work.

We built our own NAAFI club, using yet another basha and this was lined with varnished, split bamboo. A jukebox was installed, along with a separate lockable bar, with cooking facilities and secure beer storage. Lighting was put in, tables and chairs arrived and all in all, it was a grand job, very much to the credit of Bob Grey and John Green, who'd supervised the whole set up and, in some cases, worked on it themselves.

We weren't the only ones to use this facility. There was a RAF monitoring station somewhere on Penang Hill and the men of that unit had been given the go-ahead to use our bar.

Apart from downtown, there was nowhere else for them to get a drink, now that the JRC was closed to them. Aside from one individual who played one record, again and again, as shall be recorded, they never bothered us at all, and we got on well with them. Staffing this establishment were two Chinese and one young Malay boy. One of the Chinese was called Scouse for some reason, and the other, Speedy, due no doubt to his unhurried way of getting around. The small boy was called Tulip, often mispronounced as Chewlips.

After our move to the other end of camp, a four-man Uniflote crew arrived from Singapore, from 10 Port Operating Squadron RCT. The Uniflote is an engine driven, manoeuvrable raft capable of carrying heavy loads. The whole ensemble, along with the crew and numerous Gurkha wives and kids had been conveyed from Singapore aboard the LSL Sir Percivale and arrived at Georgetown docks. The units were put over the side and after a struggle in a seaway, were put together.

Pete Owen, being the engineer, got the engine firing and they set off. Going across to the landing stage at RAF Glugor, the engine failed, putting them at risk as they were in the ferry track. Pete eventually got the engine going again and they brought the Uniflote in safely. The first night there, Maurice Winter, one of the crew, incensed at being sent to Penang when he wanted to be with his girl Mary in Singapore, punched a hole in the wall of his billet and was subsequently charged. High authority didn't sympathise with him although we did.

With Maurice were two corporals, Brian Manning and Pete Owen and another driver, Brian Mahoney. This section of the RCT was an unknown quantity to me. I'd never heard of Uniflotes, Mexiflotes or the array of maritime craft they operated. All I knew about the RCT was that they were once the RASC and drove trucks around. The RASC was a favourite during National Service days for employing all the young men from our neighbourhood in London and putting them in uniform. I got on well with the RCT drivers and Uniflote crews, as they were all excellent blokes.

I met Maurice five years later in Marchwood, on the Sir Lancelot (of Falkland's fame) at the first boat drill. He was in charge of that section of the ship. He, like me, was a full corporal. Neither of us could believe meeting up again like that. On the way to Central America and over the two-week passage, we reminisced over some beers and had a lot of laughs. Sadly, Maurice died while I was writing this book.

Maurice Winter RCT
Friend and comrade

I well remember the first time I went to dinner. The cook, a bespectacled lad named Malcolm was waiting for us and asked me what I would like to eat, steak or trout. I looked him up and down and asked him if he was taking the piss, but he was adamant and asked me again if I wanted steak or trout. We were all asked our preferences as we came in. It didn't take us long to realise that food-wise, having the Gurkhas in the camp had been the best thing that could have happened. I didn't have to eat salad every day, as I'd done in Singapore. We'd really fallen on our feet. We ate like lords from then on and Malcolm and his oppo were our bosom-buddies.

Malcolm and his mate, who gave me some faith in armed forces cooks

It was a fact that the army came bottom of the pecking order where rations were concerned, and I can only guess that their standard of culinary expertise was also down there. Malcolm was a good chef and I started to put on weight. Not only that, but I also now enjoyed my food and didn't just eat to stay alive. We still got salad but this time as an accompaniment and not as a main course and Gordon could eat without relinquishing half his meal to me.

We weren't on the same ration scale as the Gurkhas and I wondered where our food came from and who the purchaser was.

Whoever fulfilled that function did a great job. Our largest complement was twenty five single men, RE, RCT, RAOC and at one stage, a RAVC member and it couldn't have been easy to find the right type of food and at the right price. I know because as an NCO, while in another squadron and on detachment, I had the difficult job of trying to buy food and not go over budget.

Now, it's a sad fact that although when in town we were surrounded by cheap food outlets, we seldom ate out at the beginning of our time in that camp. We did branch out a bit later but initially we just weren't adventurous and preferred the cooking that we were used to but on one occasion, after a load of beer, we all went to the Chinese restaurant at the Boston Bar, on Penang Road.

Someone must have ordered but for the life of me, I wouldn't know who. What arrived on the table was a big bowl of soup, which was served out and I spooned into mine and came up with a long, green, slimy thing. I asked no one in particular 'what the f*** is this?' and Scouse Gore said it was what they tested the fat with. I wasn't hungry after that.

I've since found out that what we had then was mee-hoon soup and what was in my food was some sort of cooked vegetable, but I didn't know this at the time.

I called him a Scouse bastard and thanked him for ruining my meal, whereat the whole table fell about laughing, especially Gordon, who said now I knew how he felt back in Singapore. (The biter bit!) There had been a war of words between Scouse and me since Broadbridge Heath days, each of us trying to provoke the other into taking some action, without success. To me he was 'You Scouse bastard' and to him, I was a 'little Cockney c***'.

When we did eat out and it was seldom, we ate at the mankiest Indian restaurant imaginable, the Craven A, so called because of the cigarette advertisement on the roof. There, we ate beef curry and rice. The place was old and knocked about but served a good, cheap curry.

They had a toilet there and it was well used, obviously, with all the boozy patrons coming in. The toilet consisted of a couple of sheets of galvanised iron set up just off the kitchen but with the passage of time and thousands of gallons of urine, the metal was peppered with holes, and I've seen someone peeing there and spray coming through the holes and going into the full chatties of rice on the kitchen floor.

We saw it and ignored it, knowing that we'd got our food before this happened and in our boozed-up condition, forgetting that it had been going on before we arrived.

In all my years of living in the East and eating curry, I've never tasted one in a curry shop to compare with the

Craven A. Despite the unsanitary conditions, none of us suffered from eating there! No sudden trips to the toilet in the middle watches, no stomach aches. It must have been good as there were always plenty of diners there. I'm not saying I'd take my wife there to dine but it served us well at the time.

After eating our curry, we then had the job of finding a taxi to take us back to Minden Barracks. This wasn't always easy. The local cab driving fraternity had suffered badly at the hands of 2 RGJ and possibly even their predecessors and had built up a healthy distrust of anyone wishing to go to the camp, sober or otherwise. They'd had passengers who turned violent, passengers who'd refused point blank to pay and they'd seen their fares leap from the taxi and run laughing, hooting and shouting into the night and impossible to find.

They had grown very wary about carrying soldiers, especially drunks, back to Minden. Until we proved otherwise, we were treated with grave distrust too. At one stage the taxi used to stop at the guardroom, where we had to pay up, before he would proceed any further. I saw all this repeated in Singapore but at a level that left Minden Barracks in the junior league.

At Gillman Barracks, they'd elevated taxi driver aggravation and fare dodging to an art form. (Imagine a galvanised dustbin, loaded with rubble, being dropped onto your cab from a height of about forty feet. That's what they did at Gillman Barracks! It's lucky the poor bloody taxi driver wasn't sitting inside)

There was to be a wedding! Bob Grey was getting married to his German girlfriend, Aneka. John Green was the best man and the rest of us went to give the bridegroom much needed support in his ordeal. The ceremony took place at St Georges church and it all went off smoothly.

The reception was given by the OC and his wife, at their home. It was a good spread and well received and it was unusual in that we all got to see inside an officer's home.

Dumping started in late July. I shan't forget my first sight of bombs. They were rusty, unimpressive chunks of metal but just one of these had the potential of sending us all to bomb disposal heaven, should there be such a place and we'd better remember it. We handled them accordingly at first. As we grew accustomed to them, our attitude changed; not blasé but more relaxed. After all, one of these things could go up whether being handled roughly or gently and we knew it. Providing we stood right next to it, we weren't going to feel a thing.

I maintain this attitude wasn't bravado; it was an honest appraisal of the situation. We'd discussed all this in our off-duty moments and unanimously declared that although none of us wanted to end up as a name on the Bomb Disposal Roll of Honour, instant annihilation was better than maiming or permanent disability. We didn't share this opinion with our bosses because they'd probably have thought we had a morale problem.

Our first load was ready for conveying to RAF Glugor. A 3-tonner was loaded up with 60kg bombs, which were heavily sandbagged round and then we set off. The OC led, in his Land Rover and two Malay motorcycle policemen rode as escort. Brian Ridley was driving the truck and I was in the front with him. I got a bit carried away with the drama and I was standing on the engine cowling with my body through the cupola, wearing beret and goggles when Brian shouted up to me to bloody well sit down and did I think I was bloody Rommel? It quite destroyed the moment!

We arrived at Glugor and the bombs were unloaded onto the Uniflote, which then set off for the LCT, (landing craft tank). There were four LCT's in the fleet, based in Singapore. These were the Arromanches, Arakan, Antwerp and the Ardennes. The two used the most were the Arromanches and the Arakan and I spent some memorable hours on these two. Using these vessels had caused some heart-searching at their base in Singapore. To be safe, we needed two vessels each time a dumping run was considered; one for us and the bombs and another in case of an explosion. The secondary vessel had to be large enough to carry all the LCT and RE crews, should there be any survivors. To use two LCT's each time would halve 33 Maritime's capability and so an RAF rescue launch was to be provided on Tuesdays and Thursdays and we had to adjust our work practices to suit.

The bombs were put on a pallet, three at a time, and lifted by the LCT's derrick onto the catwalk. This was the time when some bombs did get bumped. Getting them off the pallet and upright meant a little rough handling because only one man could do the job due to lack of space. Two other team members stood ready with ropes and tackle. Stevedores from the crew helped with the work, raising the pallets and directing the loading. Our load for this first run was eighty 60kg bombs, about five tons in weight and it took us one and a half hours to load the LCT.

When ready, the LCT set off for the dumping grounds. It wasn't a smooth run and was done during the monsoon season and the craft bucked and rolled, and we on the catwalk got soaked. We had one case of seasickness and I can remember the poor wretch hanging over the side, but the LCT crew had more sea-sickness cases!

The only cure for this problem is dry land and that wouldn't be for hours and until we returned and docked, it was just a case of head down and suffer. The bad weather caused the trip to take four hours. It was still blowing when the dumping commenced.

There were four of us and we paired off and picked up the bombs, one hand each on the tail fin and the other holding a sandbag under the bomb's nose. After one backward swing we launched the bombs overboard. One thing we hadn't foreseen was the tendency of the bombs to curve in towards the ship's side, but we were made aware of this when the bomb hit the hull and there was a dull 'thump' throughout the ship and a few hearts jumped. The vessel's captain told us to stop work while they reconsidered. I can only imagine now how that man felt at the time. Thirty miles offshore, in a monsoon and with a million pounds of vessel and should we survive the explosion when the ship went down, about 30 people under his care.

The order came for us to throw them further out. We did this but with the same result and we had some bad moments, waiting for the explosion that would sink the ship and end everything. It never happened, of course, but it so easily could have done. It was obvious that a different method of disposal was needed but at that time, we had only arm power and so we carried on but exerted ourselves, obeyed the captain and threw them as far out as we could.

This was not only the first trip but for me, almost the last as well. Some of the bombs had damaged tail fins and while throwing a bomb with Jim Stow, a curled section of broken tail fin caught my left wrist and took me over the side. I shouted and with great presence of mind and even greater speed, Bob Nesbitt threw one arm around my waist and grabbed the back of my shorts with the other. The bomb tore itself free, dropping into the ocean. I was badly cut about the wrist but better that than a thirty fathom watery grave. Thank you Bob, from the bottom of my heart.

We came back from that first dumping trip in the RAF launch, which travelled at about thirty knots. It could go faster but there was a bit of a sea running due to the monsoon. During this trip back, our sea-sickness patient had to go through it all again. He sat with his head hanging down, not daring to look at the sea rushing past.

The launch was leaping from wave to wave and all of us felt a bit queasy at times. I found that being below was better than being on deck. Below I couldn't see the horizon jumping about.

On the next run, a wooden chute was used that had been constructed, to allow the bombs to slide easily off into deep water and it worked admirably. With the forward end of the chute supported by a derrick, eighty 60kg bombs could be dumped in ten minutes, into thirty fathoms. Apparently, there was an equal amount of mud on the bottom, so the bombs would be entombed. The LCT Captain wasn't the only one to breathe a sigh of relief at the change or procedure. We were only too aware of what might have happened.

Picrate crystals on the outside of the bomb cases could easily have ignited by rubbing against metal and it can only be the fact that it took place under water that stopped any reaction.

There was considerable trouble dumping the 250kg bombs. Too big to go down our chute, two of them were dropped overboard through the bow doors by a tractor. Dave Woolmer recalls that he was driving the little Ferguson forklift tractor and had a bomb resting on the forks. He had to go right to the edge of the ramp before tipping the bomb into the sea and he felt very unsafe. This method was stopped because the vessel's captain was worried that the tractor would hit and damage the doors. The only alternative we had then was for the ship's derrick to lift each bomb by rope and then the rope was cut. Dave later found that the life jacket he'd been given was useless, so he had every reason to be concerned. Later, a larger chute was constructed that would take the bigger bombs.

Coming back from that dumping trip, I stayed on deck. Even when ashore, I was never one for playing cards, which the rest of them were doing. The weather had calmed down and I enjoyed being at sea. The thought did cross my mind that I should have enlisted in the Royal Navy. I liked it so much that I put in for a transfer to the RCT, stipulating that

I wanted to go to RCT Maritime and intended to become a marine engineer.

My comrades were disgusted with my course of action, but it was my life, not theirs. As night approached, the phosphorescence of the ship's wake glowed. I thought it was a magical sight and much better than sitting below and looking at bulkheads.

On another dumping run, we'd got rid of the bomb load and clambered onto the RAF launch and settled aboard. The engines were started up, only to be immediately shut down again. Something was stopping the launch from moving. Two of the crew were diver trained and they put their kit on and went over side to investigate.

A cable had somehow wrapped itself round the prop shaft and it took repeated dives to free it. This held us up for about an hour and the launch used almost full throttle on its return journey, touching about thirtyfive knots. With no sea running, it was a good trip although our sea-sickness patient wouldn't have agreed with me.

In many respects, our leadership did not make a good impression on the RCT, nor on our team members and who can blame them? Many had served in BAOR and other places and had 'been around the block'. One had served in Cyprus, Hong Kong and along the Mediterranean coast and I don't think he was too impressed, being ex-RE. Being wholly professional, they weren't blind to the sometimes weird actions or thought processes of our bosses.

One was the RCT Movement Control Corporal, Ken Brett, another ex-RE. Ken didn't work with us but with the Malay 402 Troop RCT. He shared our accommodation and NAAFI facilities, and it was he who re-christened the task from Operation Bombs Penang to Big Bangs Penang, thereby taking the wind out of its sails. Big Bangs Penang it was from then on.

Ken Brett RCT
Known as Tuan Besar
(Malay for Big Boss)

I met Ken twice more, in 1972 and 1975 and he still referred to it the same way. I don't wish to give the wrong impression about this.

Although most of us had a fierce pride in our unit and the badge we wore (esprit de corps, they call it), we couldn't expect others to follow suit. It was no use us getting upset at the jibes directed at the unit, which was all in good fun anyway.

British soldiers get used to the never-ending inter-unit rivalry although it has led to serious trouble, and I can recall as a recruit when it led to death at Aldershot NAAFI Club and has been known to need the intervention of a whole regiment of RMP'S.

No such trouble reared its ugly head between the RCT and RE components; we got along very well. Some of our colleagues had served for a number of years and no doubt looked on us as youngsters, to be tolerated. Ken was such a one. Although only a Lance Corporal, he'd served in our corps before being re-badged as RCT. Another was Brian Manning, the Uniflote skipper. Brian had already done years with the RE, in 17 Port Operating Squadron before being re-badged and had been to places we'd only heard of. Brian was not at all happy at having been made to relinquish his RE badge for that of the RCT and wasn't backward about saying so but he was a professional soldier and got on with his job, doing it well.

A professional seaman, courtesy of the RE, he'd been to Hong Kong and had once been part of a team on a RCT Z Craft that had to tow a Heavy Floating Bridge (HFB) from Cyprus to Libya. After a nightmare voyage, nursing the HFB along the coast in bad weather, they got it just off the Libyan coast, where it promptly sank. I was considered at twenty-two to be one of the more mature team members and Brian was three years my senior so the younger members of our gang were like kids to him.

Our average day didn't start with any sort of reveille. We were all old enough to know that we had to be on parade, and it was left to us to make sure we were. Those going to breakfast were up at about 06:45 to enable them to get to the cookhouse and back in time for parade. It was a long walk.

I preferred to have an extra half hour in bed and the first cigarette of the day; an awful habit but one my body recognised. There was an archaic law in the army that decreed we had to attend breakfast. At one stage, troops were marched to breakfast in a body. What happened when they got to the cookhouse and to those who didn't want or wouldn't eat the food, I don't know. After all, you can't force a man to eat if he doesn't want to.

My attendances at breakfast during my ten years in the army could have been counted on both hands. At 07:45, we paraded on the strip of weeds that fronted the office, had a roll-call and were detailed off for the day's tasks. We didn't all work together. On dumping day, most of the team would go to the site to dig while half a dozen took the bombs away to be loaded on the Uniflote and then the LCT. I always preferred the dumping run to digging, but we did have to take it in turn. If there was no dump, we all went to the site and either drilled with the Proline, used hand augers or dug bombs out.

I was invited to go to Malacca for the weekend with Jim Land and Dave Woolmer. It had to be a flight as there wasn't time to drive there. The airfare was fifty Malay dollars return and I even had to borrow that! We left Penang Airport and the flight to Malacca took a mere forty-five minutes. I was given a bed in 3 Squadron's lines and that afternoon, went with Jim, Dave and some others to a bar and had too much to drink. On getting back to 3 Squadron, I crashed out on the bed. I was invited out that evening but decided to have another hour's sleep but went out later to Terendak's Beach Club with Nat Barclay and Dave Taylor. We had a few beers and walked back. On the way we were accosted by a dozen Aussies from 1 RAR, who were out to pick a fight, didn't matter who with. Nat traded punches with one of these idiots and then we carried on to 3 Squadron's line. There were hundreds of Aussies at RAAF Butterworth, and they had a club on Penang and drank in the same bars as us but they never acted like those idiots in Malacca.

The Australian infantry have been touted as among the best fighting soldiers in the world and so they may be but those ones I met were ignorant and stroppy and they didn't like the English. I suspect that they might have been conscripts, the bottom of the military food chain, with limited intelligence and a grudge against a world that had made them leave their homes. Nat said that this sort of thing was a regular occurrence.

The powers that be now thought it was high time we had some sort of fitness test and in lieu of a BFT, a climb up Penang Hill was chosen. There's an adequate road that goes to the top, and it takes about three hours to hike it, but we went up the hard way, climbing through the lower scrub and then thicker jungle higher up. From a distance, Penang Hill looks very much like any other hill, but it was cloaked in surprisingly thick jungle, broken up by ravines and waterfalls. You could get lost there. Not irretrievably lost as in some other places in the Malayan jungle but lost for a good few hours.

We'd been paraded and checked. We all wore jungle hats, jackets, long trousers, jungle boots, each had a golok and a filled water bottle. We were driven to the base of the hill, off loaded and told to set off. A few of us had been drinking heavily in the NAAFI the night before and I for one, felt very queasy. It was a scorching hot day and the sweat was pouring from us but that was all to the good and I felt fine after I'd got rid of the beer inside me.

The way was steep, and we made progress only by catching hold of shrubs and saplings and pulling ourselves up. I don't recall how long it took to get to the car park near the summit, which was our destination but we finally all made it. Greeny had been back marker, making sure none of us was bitten by a snake or attacked by hornets or anything else that lurked in the vicinity. He rallied us and kept us going up, and ever up.

We must have made it in the allotted time or we'd no doubt have found ourselves back there again the next day.

The car park where we gathered was something of a tourist area and had the usual cafe and bar and before we went back down the hill, we headed there to replace in beer what we'd lost in sweat.

JOHN GREEN

Greeny went to Chepstow in 1960 and left there in 1962. From there he went to Cove for basic training. He was posted to 26 Armoured Engineer Sqn at Hohne. Hated it, bloody tanks! (his words).

For some misdemeanour, he was given 14 days detention in the Hussars guardroom and while there was told by someone awaiting court martial that the best way to get out of a squadron was to apply to join 9 Para, the RE parachute squadron. A failure there meant a posting but not back to the one you'd left. He duly applied and was sent to 9 Sqn's base at Aldershot. He was given 14 days detention there but what for I have no idea but he did engineer this himself. After that he was posted to Broadbridge Heath, where he sat his bomb disposal course and passed out top of the course.

The RSM then sent him on a JNCO's cadre at Cove in which he again came top. He was a blacksmith/welder by trade and a formidable rugby player. He always told us that we'd find life in a field squadron very different from the life we knew in Bomb Disposal, and he said some of us would find it difficult to adjust.

This was correct but not in the way John meant. Being BD engineers, most field squadrons had no use for us and we ended up with other jobs.

He never pushed his rank when dealing with us and we looked on him as a mate. In my opinion he was a good lance jack. John stayed in the army and did his full term and as far as I know, finished as a Sgt Major.

There's been a lot of talk about the temperature increasing far beyond what it was in the past, but in 1967 it was hot in Penang. We watched rubber trees explode due to the heat; spontaneous combustion, it's called. We assumed that the raw latex got beyond its critical flashpoint and couldn't

LCpl John Green
Port Eynon

think of any other rational explanation. We knew how hot it was because we were working outside and not all the sites were in the shade.

There wasn't an ounce of fat on me, and most of the lads were the same, light and stringy. Working in those temperatures ensured we stayed thin, but we were fit and needed to be, so the hike up Penang Hill was considered necessary. None of us suffered from it and all felt better for doing it. A BFT it wasn't but it was at least an indication that we were in fairly good physical condition.

Chapter Twelve

Having settled in nicely, some of us took to hobbies of various sorts. Tim Vismer made model airplanes and the final one, made in August, was the biggest and the best. It was a plastic Junkers 87 Stuka, complete with engine and a wingspan of about two feet. On test day we all assembled outside our basha to watch the inaugural flight. Tim proudly brought the model out and prepared it. The ailerons were tested, fuel tank topped up, engine started and then the thing took off. Tim handled it well, twiddling the knobs of the control unit. He took it up and then put it into the classic Stuka dive. Down it came, almost vertically and Tim moved the control to bring it out of the dive and the bloody thing never responded. Straight down it went, onto hard, sun-baked earth and almost disintegrated. I felt sorry for Tim. He'd spent a lot of time and money on that model. Back to the drawing board!

TIM VISMER

Big Tim Vismer was a nice lad. Born in Rhodesia, he'd been in the army there, but as a conscript. He was very much a 'white' Rhodesian and had no love for those who ruined what he considered to be his country. His family moved to the Cape and from there Tim went to England and enlisted in the RE.

He was generally a quiet bloke but could be roused! I recall him going for me after I once called him a Kaffir! I found him to be well educated and well spoken.

Tim put himself into his job and was at the forefront of work in Penang. He was a good friend and seldom downhearted and he and I stayed together by being posted to the same squadron in Singapore.

He remained a lance jack. He left the army after six years' service and he visited me at Longmoor in 1972 but I've never heard of him since.

Big Tim Vismer
May 1968

I'm not sure of the sequence or date of the next incidents but they throw some light on how we spent our time. One of the lads started going into Georgetown alone and he took to frequenting the same 'knocking shop' on every visit. He went there so often and was obviously such a valued customer that the owner invited him round to his house for Sunday lunch.

One night, just as I was drifting off to sleep, I heard a 'toot-toot' coming from way out in the blackness. It came again and again 'toot-toot, toot-toot'. Tim woke up and asked what the hell was going on. I said I didn't know but I was going to find out. So, I got up and went outside and Tim joined me. Coming toward us was a strange figure. It was carrying a lighted candle, wearing a huge coolie hat, and was blowing on a flute. It was one of the team, but I won't mention which one. He was stoned out of his mind. I got rid of the hat, which would have disgraced a scarecrow and we took him in the basha, undressed him and after putting him on his bed, threw his mosquito net over him.

Next morning the lad was totally incapable and couldn't even get out of bed. John Green came in just before parade, and we told him what had happened. Greeny took in the situation straight away; he told our drunk to stay where he was, closed the wooden shutters and the door, leaving him in the room. We went on parade. How John explained a team member's absence from the parade and worksite and managed to keep George Duncan and the OC from finding out we never knew.

That night, after we got back from work, we heard the full story. He'd gone to the usual place and been introduced to the owner's pals. They'd plied him with toddy and got him smoking pot. Greeny gave him a good 'ear bashing' and read him the riot act about the dangers of using drugs and drinking stuff like toddy. John had risked his rank by keeping him under wraps.

Had he not done so, there would surely have been a charge of being drunk on parade. And questions might well have been asked by the Military Police about drugs. The man involved may have forgotten all about this incident and if he hasn't, he may not wish for friends and family to know what happened so his identity is safe with me.

Toddy is a drink made from the secretions of the flowers of the coconut palm. It's cheap to produce and costs a few dollars a litre, which is usually sold in plastic bottles. It's whitish in colour and has a slight tang of lemons when it's at its best. My father was blind drunk on this stuff during the war while in Sierra Leone and ended up in front of 'the captain's table', 'Jackspeak' for being on a charge. I drunk a quart of it a few years ago and it had little effect. It must have been watered down, or a bad batch maybe. Apparently, it's the last resort of the winos in Malaysia.

One Sunday morning Bob Nesbitt was full of his experiences of the night before. He'd been in town and gone to the Soo Chow Hotel, which doubled as a knocking shop, and he was ecstatic about the girl he'd been with. He said to me that the next time I wanted my end away, I should ask there for Chinese Annie, because she's a good shag and I should tell her I'm a friend of Irish Bob. I replied that they're all bleedin' Chinese and suppose there's more than one named Annie. What then? He assured me all would be well.

Scouse Gore we hardly ever saw in off duty hours. He'd got his feet under the table down at RAF Glugor and spent practically every night there. He'd been a bit of a drinker back in England, but now had the opportunity to give his hobby full rein.

**Jim 'Scouse' Gore on
board LCT Ardennes**
June 1967

He did me a favour though. There was a dance being held at Glugor and Scouse asked me if I'd design and draw a poster for it. I made him a poster, ornamented around the edges by cartoons of The Perishers, the comic strip of the time from the Daily Mirror. The favour he did was getting me to do it in the rainy season, thereby giving me something to do.

We were very much confined to camp for days on end because of the heavy rain. The poster was considered good enough to be auctioned off at the end of the dance, a dance none of us were invited to incidentally; something we'd remember for the future! Even our bosses thought the poster was amusing and I was allowed to see it through. Having Farrow in the office drawing was better than Farrow being on his bed with a book.

These days were something of a trial; the sites were a sea of mud. We were no strangers to mud and had that been the only issue, I'm sure we'd have been out working. But, one Proline was in REME workshops, along with the bomb locators. The locators spent a lot of time in workshops. They'd been made and designed to operate in temperate conditions and here they received a lot of heat and rough handling.

I suppose another round of tool cleaning could have been implemented but there's only so much in the way of tool maintenance that anyone can do. They weren't being used much so weren't getting dirty. We'd cleaned, polished, sharpened and oiled them to within an inch of their lives. The heavy machinery had likewise been cleaned down, waiting for better weather.

I don't recall how it came about but I went to a children's home in Georgetown in the company of the OC's wife. She was very upper class and true to her type, never did a stroke of work; her forte' was charity. This kid's home covered a large area and in the garden, they had a big aviary, with many budgerigars and other small birds. They bred so many budgies that the aviary was getting overcrowded, and they started selling them off.

I bought a large cage from them and three birds. I told them that I wanted to see if they'd settle down in our room before I bought more. They did settle and I said I'd buy more.

So, at a later date, Jenny, the OC's wife, drove to camp and in her cut-glass accent, called for me and asked if I was there. Of course I was bloody there! Where did she think I was going to be? I went to the home in the Loch's Mk 7 Jag. I enjoyed being driven around in that. Jenny Loch, a big, statuesque, blondish woman was alright and quite good looking, but I always had the impression that she'd much rather be somewhere else or with someone else. I bought three more birds, and everything went well for a few months.

I came back from work one day and I found two of the birds dead in the bottom of the cage and the others scared almost to death. The dead ones hadn't a mark on them and must have died of fright. Someone said that they'd seen a big cat prowling round the rooms, so I had my culprit. I borrowed Tim's spear gun and went looking for this cat (we were plagued with feral cats) but instead of meeting the cat, I met George Duncan, who asked me what I was doing with the gun. I told him and he said that if I shot the cat, he'd put me on a charge.

No worries about dead budgies, you notice, just about a scabby cat! I should have said 'Yes Sarge' and waited for him to leave before recommencing my hunt. If I'd found the thing, I'd have skewered it to the nearest tree. It's the thing to do with vermin.

One night we had a mighty storm and the wet weather resulted in termites swarming. Thousands poured out of a hole in a tree near our showers, thousands of yellow wriggling bodies, known as alates, about half an inch long. They shed their wings and covered the ground. Tim and Mick scooped them up by the handful and filled their mouths. There were shouts of disgust; they were told they were bloody animals, to turn it in, pack it up and generally cease forthwith. Tim explained that they tasted like butter. They might well have done but I prefer to get my butter in a packet stamped Anchor. It was a disgusting sight! I can understand a bushman doing it because he has to, but I can't think what makes a white man eat grubs when he has a perfectly adequate canteen nearby.

We drank in several bars in Georgetown but did have a preference for three, the Tiger Bar on Chulia Street, another on Beach Road whose name escapes me and the Pathe Bar near the Esplanade. Earlier we had done numerous recces and visited most bars, some of which we didn't like, some were too far away and some had no girls. We settled on these three as they were what we were looking for and made friends with the girls in two of them. The Tiger Bar was good in that it had up to date records on the jukebox, The Beatles being a favourite. This was the time of I am the Walrus, All you need is Love, Hullo, Goodbye plus San Francisco, The Mamas and Papas, along with Nancy Sinatra and Lee Hazelwood and other well-known western artistes.

One night, Bob Nesbitt and a member of the Uniflote crew met in the Tiger Bar and were accosted by a lady of the night, who suggested they go back to her place, and she'd accommodate them both. Very unusual this and they readily agreed to it and went with her. In her bedroom, while they were shedding clothes, she mentioned the price of this service, which had them both dressed and out of the door in record time!

The Beach Road bar had no jukebox but did have a record player and a decent collection of LPs and it was usually staffed by one lone Chinese girl, who served beer but didn't fraternise. It was a strange looking bar; the décor was white tiles, very much like a public toilet. Gordon found a record there that took his fancy, a Seekers LP entitled A World of Our Own and there was one song he liked more than any other, The Leaving of Liverpool. I can only guess this song held something special for him. He hailed from Accrington, in Lancashire, so Liverpool was not too far from his home. He'd left behind a girl named Jean and maybe she came from there.

It was a private matter, and no one asked. We used this strange bar quite often but after a period of absence, we went there, and it had closed.

GORDON WHIPP

Gordon was an amusing character; bespectacled and blonde haired, with a very gruff voice, he had a wry sense of humour. If he had any interests outside drinking, I never knew them. He never chased after the girls and was saving himself for his Jean, who he intended to marry when he got home. He could be relied on to tell funny stories in his Lancashire accent and was one of those people who fit in anywhere.

He'd been on Operation Nutcracker, the Radfan road building campaign and had some interesting stories to tell about his service there. Life would have been very different if he hadn't been a part of the team. Gordon left the army and moved to South Africa. He lived near Johannesburg and set up a business as a cutler, producing top-of-the-range knives. I corresponded with him for a few years and had one phone call with him. He died in 2016.

Gordon at the Ocean Inn, Penang
April 1967

Brian Manning, the skipper of the Uniflote crew, suggested the novel idea of having a weekly al fresco booze and record session and we jumped at the chance. The site chosen was in front of our basha. At the first sitting there were about half a dozen of us, but this swelled to a dozen or more when the word got round. Scouse had a prized collection of records, many of which I'd never heard.

This was the first time that any of us had heard the Sgt Pepper album and although it was weird compared to conventional music, I liked it. George Harrison playing the sitar was a first and the Indian music was in keeping with our current lifestyle then, as we were surrounded by Indians and their music. Enough chairs were found, and we sat at a table taken from our room. A galvanised dustbin was cleaned out, filled with ice from the bar and we all chipped in and loaded up the bin with cans of Tiger beer.

Scouse played his records and we all got drunk while singing along to the records. Scouse alternated the records with jokes and stories, and he was the life and soul. His rendition of a Pakistani was NOT pc but had us falling about laughing. He would have made an excellent DJ! I've seen some of my mates slide from their chair onto the grass, a full can in one hand, cigarette in the other and just sit there, blank eyed and staring but still listening.

If I close my eyes, I can still hear Scouse and others of those voices down the years. It was a long time later that I even understood the lyrics to Sgt Pepper. I had more fun while NOT understanding! Playing those songs now brings back so many intense memories that it's difficult to settle down afterwards. Oh, to be young again!

Brian's reason for suggesting the move outside was due to a moronic RAF type who time and time again, played one record on our jukebox, 'A Whiter Shade of Pale'. No amount of persuasion would get him to play something else for a change and he persisted with playing this record. Brian said he was getting a bit homicidal about this cretin, who should have been a resident of Netley Military Hospital (the army's loony bin!)

In retrospect, we ought to thank this idiot, as we had a far better time drinking outside than we ever did in the NAAFI. However, we didn't look at it in that light at the time. A good thumping may have shown the fool the error of his ways, but we couldn't honestly do that. While the RAF had taken no part in the construction and fitting out of the NAAFI, we'd agreed to share it with them and so we had to tolerate their shortcomings. It was a democratic society we lived in, and he was entitled to play whatever he wanted, even while it drove us mad!

At one stage, the bomb loading location had to be changed from Glugor to the very south of the island, at Batu Maung. The reason for this was because the ramp at Glugor was closed down for a month to enable repairs to be made. Some of our personnel, to whit, John Green, Bob Nesbitt and Scouse Gore, worked on the ramp repairs, concreting. It was very hot working there, no shade to speak of and with the sun bouncing off the concrete.

Someone with no thought to the consequences, had given the keys of the place to Greeny. This included the keys to the bar. The three of them helped themselves to booze and one day, George Duncan turned up, saw them drinking and had a complete sense of humour failure. (George was not a drinker!) He could get drunk on a couple of cans of cider.

Batu Maung was chosen as it had a beach for easy access and the Uniflote could get in fairly close to the shore. Unlike Glugor, a RAF base, which was closed and secure, Batu Maung was wide open and our arrival with military vehicles was soon noted and our efforts at moving bombs from trucks to the Uniflote were closely observed by the locals, who lined the road, squatting for hours in the sun watching to see what the 'round eyes' were up to.

The bombs were in full view, each one carried by two soldiers from the truck out onto the craft. It would have been interesting to question some of those locals present and ask them how much explosive they'd bought for fish bombing purposes. Batu Maung back then was just a fishing village and I'm sure that the fishermen there were no strangers to using the filling of the bombs from the sites we were working on. Had the locals not dug up bombs for this purpose, it's doubtful if the authorities would have been aware of the presence of so many bombs on the island. They would have been mightily surprised in the future when extensive development work was carried out. Sungai Nibong was transformed from a sleepy village to a bustling community with multi high-rise apartment blocks and all traces of the former rubber plantations had disappeared. So it was with the sites at Sungai Dua, Bukit Gedong and the sites north of Georgetown.

Digging out the bombs

Loading the Uniflote

Uniflote ready to cast off

Full load approaching the LCT

Rose with sling, Farrow loading the pallet

Nesbitt, Farrow and Rose, loading up

All were flattened and built over. The sites at Sungai Dua became home to the ramps for the first Penang Bridge. The former Minden Barracks, now the Malaysian Science University, is dwarfed by the bridge structure. There was speculation among the troops, if not the hierarchy, whether we'd left anything dangerous behind but I'm sure that we'd have heard if anything had been found.

Mick Rose was an easy-going young man. Born in Kenya, his family had moved back to England after Mick's mother had been murdered by the Mau Mau. I think they owned a farm back there, but the situation had become untenable with

Mick Rose

the rise of this terrorist group and they left for a safer place. Mick was a hard worker and although only twenty, could also be a hard drinker when he chose. He mixed in well with everyone and was seldom downhearted. When he visited us one evening in Singapore, he was an instant success with my wife for offering to dry the dishes after our meal.

We had to have words with our sergeant. To him, I was Farrow, Scouse was Gore and each and every one was called by his surname, except Tim Vismer.

Tim was called Tim! We asked why and were told that he'd known Tim since he (George) was a corporal and they were friends. Out of order, we told him. We had to abide by military rules, so sergeants should do likewise, and George was reminded that military etiquette dictated that we should all be treated equally, something he as a sergeant should have known. Although I refer to him by Christian name here, he was only ever called sergeant by us. He got grumpy about our attitude and called it childish, but we had a point and insisted. (Tim was an embarrassed bystander while this was going on).

From then on, Tim was referred to as Vismer but for a short while only. Tim was given his first stripe. Good for him and we were happy for him. In retrospect, this might well have been George's answer to our complaint but if it was, it backfired. We made sure that George now called Tim, Cpl Vismer. Tim bought the beers that night in the NAAFI, as per tradition. Bomb Disposal was long known as a place where promotion was hard to get and generally only came on the demise of a colleague; dead men's shoes! The rest of us had no hope of a stripe while in this unit but we accepted that. As a six-year regular with no intentions of signing on again, I didn't care one way or another about promotion at that time. I didn't expect it so wasn't worried.

Although we were spared general duties, we did find ourselves detailed in October and we were fortunate at being around for the Hindu festival of Dashera. The Gurkhas wanted every man of their battalion to be free to celebrate, so we had to stand guard for one day. Moans all round, which is normal, even though we hadn't done guard duty for years, not even in Singapore and never in Broadbridge Heath.

Sgt George Duncan

I was detailed off to guard a compound in the lower reaches of the camp, very near the back gate and close to an armoury. It was a painless duty, more boring than exacting and I spent my time wandering around looking at what was close at hand, which was a chain link fence, some metal hangar-type sheds and the distant hills. I have stood guard many times but never with a firearm and once again we were armed only with pick handles, so any incursion by commie bandits would have left us very dead and with nothing to show for it. More of this subject later. Even our predecessors had stood guard with only pick helves as a defence.

We couldn't honestly begrudge the Gurkha's their day off. They were a fighting battalion and earned any time off they had, and this festival was very important to them. It's a strange festival to those who have never witnessed it and not to be seen by the squeamish. Sacrifices are made, vegetables to start with, which are sliced in half by a Gurkha with a kukri.

Next come goats, whose heads are removed by one swift stroke of the knife and the culmination is a buffalo. A larger variation of the kukri is used on that and it's usual for a really beefy soldier to perform the kill and he takes the head off the buffalo with one cut. I've seen it. I have a photo of the beast just standing there, head and body separate, before toppling over. I decided not to include it. Not many westerners get the chance to witness this festival and it was mainly due to our standing their guards that we had the opportunity.

That night, they had a party. There were no women present, just the soldiers and they got paralytic on rum, singing and dancing with each other and having a tremendous time. The rum they drank was G1098 issue and packed a powerful punch and I can imagine there were a lot of sore heads the next day.

October was a busy month for us, and it heralded the arrival of another sergeant, this one to help out with administration. He was posted in from elsewhere in FARELF and I couldn't think of anyone less suited to admin than this man. His name was Sanderson. He wasn't a disciplinarian by any means and away from other SNCO's and the OC, insisted we all call him Sandy.

He was usually very friendly to us but had a down on the RCT lads for some reason and he particularly disliked Dave Woolmer and the feeling was mutual. Dave christened him BDC (Big Daft C***) but would never have called him that to his face and I don't blame him. Sandy was huge; one of the biggest men I've ever seen.

He was sent to us on 'good behaviour'. What the misdemeanour was that had caused this I never knew but from what I saw of him a couple of years later, it must have been something physical. However, he behaved himself while with us (almost) but one dark night, he and Gordon Whipp got boozed-up at Sandy's pad and then did a section attack on the Gurkha guardroom and tried to spirit away the captured Japanese machine gun that was on display outside. They were seen early on in their escapade and apprehended with little difficulty and probably gave the Gurkhas a good laugh, but it had to be reported and Sandy and Gordon found themselves in hot water next day.

Two years later I heard that Sandy was court martialled for striking an officer. I'd met Sandy on being posted to Longmoor and the story I heard was that he'd dropped the adjutant on morning parade in front of the whole squadron. It just wasn't the way to do it! But that was Sandy!

Apart from hard work, we were getting no real exercise while in the garrison. Someone had the idea that instead of us lying on our beds or going into Georgetown, we should devote Saturday mornings to some sort of team effort but were at a loss as to which one and how to put it into practice. We hadn't the talent, numbers or member interest to field a football team and as far as I can recall, there was little scope for any other proper sports.

I was never a sportsman and hated bloody football anyway, so this was no loss to me. Then British Bulldog and Murder Ball were suggested and given a try. At last I found something to get my teeth into and enjoy. I was the smallest and lightest and was therefore at some risk, but everyone was treated the same, size didn't matter, no holds were barred.

There is nothing sportsmanlike about these brutal games. British Bulldog is the school playground game of tag but played by grown men and murder ball, played with a medicine ball, is rugby without any vestige of rules and both as played by us were pure violence. Everyone apart from the OC and SNCO's took part and we could all work off our baser instincts on bringing down people we didn't like.

It's a pity that the hierarchy didn't participate as Saturday morning was one of the times, I'd be getting ready to go into town and they had stopped me from doing so and I would have enjoyed a crack at the person responsible (and without repercussions!) Obviously, this wouldn't have been the case if Sandy had taken part as there would have been repercussions and they'd probably have been physically painful. My mates knew my aversion to organised sport and Bernie Roome commented that he was surprised to see me throw myself into this with so much enthusiasm. Dressed in PT kit, we played these two violent, bone-crunching games for a few weeks and it was then stopped.

The reason given was, the Garrison QM complained that we'd emptied his store of PT vests and shorts and were destroying them faster than he could replace them. I was disappointed and it must have showed because Bernie Roome said that he could see how hard I was taking it and it was true. I'd enjoyed it. Some injuries had been expected because we weren't playing these games on the turf of Twickenham. The ground was sun-baked gravel and laterite with a few weeds thrown in and consequently, hard.

There was nothing serious, mostly sprains, bruises, cuts, grazes and ears reduced to rags but no broken bones, which is unusual. The idea of Saturday morning sports was dropped, and I was again free to do what I wanted.

After spending eight months doing our job, it was decided that we could do with a rest, and we agreed. This came under the heading of R&R and the venue for this was to be the Cameron Highlands, Malaysia's high country. We left Penang behind and headed south to Tapah, in Perak and began our winding climb up the side of a mountain.

On the way up we had a wall of undergrowth on one side and a sheer drop on the other, which got deeper and deeper until we couldn't see the bottom.

A logging truck came hurtling down the road toward us and took off our offside wing mirror. We were inches away from being sent over the edge. We found the local drivers were all of the same breed and their method of driving was accelerator hard down, limited braking and don't bother with mirrors or signals. Careful driving didn't enter into it (and still doesn't!)

On arrival at Tanah Rata, we went to our accommodation and settled in. There were only a handful of us, so it wasn't considered necessary for us to go to the usual place that the military were sent to. This was a barbed wire enclosed camp which on first sight reminded me of a POW cage. Military units on R&R used this camp and the emphasis was on fitness not rest. R&R didn't really come into it for them, and they had PT and marches. As it was roughly ten degrees cooler up there than it was at sea level, it was assumed soldiers would benefit from this exercise. We, due to our numbers, were billeted in a hotel and had to suffer no such abuse. As long as we behaved, we were given free rein. The onus was on the JNCOs to maintain discipline. We behaved. I'd never stayed in a hotel before, and I thought it was very smart and luxurious. I can recall Dave Woolmer ringing room service and ordering a bottle of whisky, which was drunk while in bed. Now that's total luxury and it's something that could never happen in a well-ordered barrack room!

Most of us went on sightseeing tours in the 3-tonner; tours that were taken very carefully after our narrow escape on the way up.

Three blokes hunted butterflies, which would have been much better photographed, instead of being pinned to a board. (Yes, I'm a wildlife conservationist.) Their trophies never lasted: the geckos which inhabited our lockers back in camp chewed lumps out of them as they'd not been properly preserved.

All I did while there was look around and take photographs, photographs of jungle, because that's mainly all there is, jungle in all sorts of colours, but still jungle. It's beautiful but it can be deadly. There's a rule there in the Blue Valley that you never stray from the path. It's one of the last unexplored rain forests on the planet, home of the Malayan tiger, the leopard, the banteng and the elephant.

So many people have been lost there forever. One in particular was an American named Jim Thompson, who'd disappeared in about March that year. He was a rich Thai silk manufacturer. He left his villa accommodation one day, went for a walk and never reappeared. It was speculated that a tiger had got him or that he'd just wandered from the path. Whatever the reason behind his disappearance he was never seen again. We stayed on the paths!

Experienced Malay soldiers have been lost for days before the Orang Asli (Original People), rescued them. Orang Asli is a fairly new name. We knew them by their old tribal name of Sakai, loin-cloth-dressed wild men living in the deep jungle; superb hunters and trackers, who used blowpipes and poison darts.

We spent a week in the Cameron's and then, just to show us that life wasn't all fun and games, we were split up and sent on jobs. Three of us, Bob Nesbitt, Bernie Roome and myself ended up at 11 Field Squadron's lines at Terendak Camp and our task was the rebuilding of a wooden jetty on the beach. I must add that Terendak covered an area of twenty-eight square miles and housed a full brigade and they had their own beach. Lucky things! We were given a felling axe, a pick and shovel, a crowbar, and a saw. Totally inadequate tools for this job.

We made a token attempt at work but had little inclination to do it anyway and spent a lot of time at The Strip, a row of bars outside the main gate. Bars with the names Wellington, Sydney, London, above them, no doubt denoting their clientele. When not out there, we had the whole of the Malacca Straits to cool off in. We were told a story while in 11 Squadron's lines that one Saturday morning, a sapper had awoken to find a huge cobra resting alongside him in his bed. Afraid to move an inch, he'd had to wait until someone else woke before he could let them know of his predicament. The snake was killed. The lines were right next to the jungle so this tale could well be true.

We had three days at Terendak and then it was back to Penang and our normal routine. Nothing was said to us about our lax performance with the wooden jetty, so obviously those in charge at Terendak didn't expect too much from us.

I met an old mate, Pete Carnighan, from training regiment, the only one who'd been posted east, I'd got friendly with a couple of lads in 11 Squadron lines that I'd meet again in the future. We enjoyed ourselves at The Strip and got a lot of sunbathing done and in the case of the other two, a lot of swimming, plus plenty of lying about on the beach, so all in all it wasn't a waste of time. There was the opportunity on Penang of swimming and sunbathing, at Batu Ferrenghi but where else could we have miles of beach to ourselves, as we had at Terendak.

Here we are, not working hard. Terendak
Oct 1967

Swimming parties were organised, as they'd been with 2 RGJ and about once a month, a truck would take troops up to Golden Sands beach at Batu Ferrenghi for a Sunday afternoon swim. I went although didn't swim. It took a good swimmer to brave the savage undertow off that beach. Even going in to chest height you could feel the tug at the ankles. We spent the afternoon lazing around and talking. Not much drinking was done on these expeditions. Drinking and swimming don't mix and with those water conditions, it wouldn't take much for someone to get lost.

So, orange juice was generally the order of the day. Crusted with salt and tired with too much sun, we'd return to camp in the truck or Land Rover in time for a shower and tea. It was at one of these swimming parties that one of the lads picked up a strange disease from the sand. Large red whorls and lumps appeared on his back, and he was hospitalised. The diagnosis was some sort of ringworm which, he was assured by the medics, would go in time. He was bedded down in an air-conditioned ward, but he never responded to treatment and as far as I know it ended up a life-long affliction. Seeing him with these lumps on his back made us wary of the beach from then on.

Someone had a good idea of unit dances. There was nowhere in camp they could be held so a different venue was required, and a proposal was put to the owners of a hotel out on the Batu Ferrenghi Road. This was Mount Pleasant. They agreed that we could hold a dance at their premises, and they would supply a bar, a bartender and music.

One Saturday night in October we were all taken out to this place. It was off the road, on the left and up a fairly steep hill and overlooked the sea. Being nighttime we could see nothing but a few lights out there. Present at this first dance were twin sisters, Sue and Mary Grundy, daughters of a REME staff sergeant. Bob Nesbitt was straight away after Sue and he spent the evening with her. I had a few dances with her sister Mary.

And then I met Karen. She was different to the others, and I was smitten! She told me her name was Karen Lim although I knew it had to be something other than Karen. Most Chinese girls adopted an English name back then (and still do!) We spent most of my free time together, even though she was living at Butterworth and I had to catch a ferry over to the mainland each time I wanted to see her.

Returning to Penang on one occasion, I fell asleep and must have made half a dozen trips, back and forth, before one of the ferry men woke me up, luckily on the Penang side. Karen introduced me to real Chinese food and during the evenings, we ate squid and green vegetables in a spicy sauce, at a small place near the waterfront. I'd never tried anything like that before.

Our pay wasn't astronomical, and my big problem back then was drinking and smoking too much. What else was there to do in a foreign garrison but drink? I seldom had much cash and Karen knew it and to my surprise, she would often buy beer for me. We made no plans for the future just then, everything was far too uncertain, but we decided we were in love and not just infatuated. It took me a while before she told me her real family name wasn't Lim at all!

We continued to see each other on Wednesday afternoons and Saturdays and whenever I could get over the water. Those afternoons I can still feel. I used to take a trishaw from the ferry to where Karen lived, feeling the hot, bright sun beating down on my back, relaxing, having a cigarette and enjoying the ride. Timeless! Going back to Minden Barracks was always an anti-climax after we'd had such a good day together and the ferry ride over the channel was undertaken in a dark frame of mind. While together we seldom did anything special. We just wandered around but she always thought I was strange because I walked about in the sun. The locals avoided the sun like the plague and with this in mind, I could usually persuade her to go to a bar for a drink, although she would only drink F&N orange and 'sarsi' (sarsaparilla).

Karen and I posing at Butterworth

I introduced her to western food, and she liked fried chicken and chips but was always wary of beef, saying it tasted too strong. On one visit to the Eden Cafe, which I must admit was very upper-crust, Karen ordered chicken and chips. Having used only chopsticks previously and unused to knives and forks, while trying to cut the chicken, it shot off the plate and went skidding across the floor. I laughed and she was embarrassed but I told her not to worry about it. I'm sure they'd seen worse! Steak and chips I ate often, both in the cookhouse and outside. I'd only ever eaten steak a few times in England! My favourite here was carpetbag steak, steak cooked with oysters inside, eaten at the Eden Café. How is it that we couldn't afford to eat like this at home and had to go to a third world country to regularly enjoy food such as steaks?

Lobster thermidor was another speciality on the Eden Café menu. Imagine eating that in Blighty! This good food was washed down with Tiger Beer or Anchor. Anchor was at times considered unfit for human consumption but it's a fact that all the famous brews in Malaysia suffered from periodic lapses in quality and what was good one month was considered unpalatable the next.

The saving grace of all these beers was their strength, which was higher than English beer. Back then bottled Guinness was 8.8 and Tiger and Anchor were 5.5 and remained so for years but now it's all 5.5 ABV. English beer by comparison was as weak as dishwater then and in many cases was still the same when I left the country in 2002. I know that with the advent of micro-breweries back in the UK, beer has changed dramatically now and all to the good. It needed to!

Chapter Thirteen

On a job like ours, accidents of any sort were bound to happen, and they were many, varied and mostly minor. Two accidents stick in my memory. One involved Dave Woolmer, one of our RCT lance jacks. He was helping with the digging and taking a shortened grip on a pick and holding it close to the pick head, he took a back-swing and stuck the point of the pick into his own head. There was blood everywhere! It looked worse than it was. He was drenched in sweat and this, mixed with the blood, poured from his head, down his face, chest and back. After he was cleaned up, he wasn't much the worse for wear, apart from a bad cut and an even worse headache.

The second incident involved me. I was standing on the edge of an area being dug out when the earth crumbled and I slid down the slope and the Bray, being operated by Ron Tobin, edged forward and caught me by the ankle, pinning me to the wall. Ron was waved back as he couldn't see what had happened. When he reversed the Bray, my leg wouldn't take my weight and I collapsed.

I was driven to the MRS at camp and after x-rays had been taken, I was admitted for observation. No bones were broken but I was told that I'd been lucky, as being so slightly built and wearing only canvas jungle boots, it wouldn't have taken much more pressure for my bone to have snapped.

I was luckier than they knew. I was caught by one of the bucket's teeth, a large, rounded piece of steel, rubbed smooth by use. Had my foot gone between the teeth, the rock-sharpened sheet steel of the bucket would no doubt have sheared off my foot.

I was bedded down in a ward and must have been light-headed because during the night I was awakened from a fever-induced nightmare and comforted by a Gurkha soldier in a wheelchair; a Gurkha who'd lost both legs. What a grand gesture from a man who was disabled for life. I've never forgotten that act of kindness and I still have a dent in the bone above my ankle to remind me of that day.

We had a lot of rain, which resulted in flooding in low-lying areas and 59 Field Squadron arrived to build a Bailey Bridge somewhere on the island. A section of the rural community had been cut off when their wooden bridge collapsed and 59 were going to remedy this.

In true field squadron fashion, the members of 59 ruined in two weeks all the goodwill we'd engendered during the preceding months. They fought, wrecking a couple of bars and stripped off and danced on tables to the song 'Zulu Warrior'. They insulted the locals and destroyed the relationship with the working girls in town, one of whom was physically assaulted. This never bothered them, as they were going back to Singapore but we had to live there.

We were not sorry to see them go and we had to try to rebuild the relationship we'd had with the bar owners and in the case of my mates, the relationship they had with the girls.

It wasn't long after this that an incident happened that stopped our job and changed the lives of many people. We were in the camp cinema on the night of the 24th November when the film stopped, the lights came on and a British Gurkha officer came in and in their own language, addressed the assembled Gurkhas. After the officer had finished, they all stood up and quietly trooped out and we wondered what the hell was going on because the Gurkhas liked their films, so for them to leave, it must have been serious. After they'd gone, the film continued.

When we got back to our lines, we found out what had caused the walkout. There had been unrest in Georgetown that day, brought about by the devaluation of the Malay dollar against the British pound and the Chinese gangs had taken the opportunity to create trouble. At that time, Georgetown was ruled by the gangs. This trouble was quickly fanned into inter-ethnic fighting and there were some deaths.

A Chinese mob confronted one lone, small figure walking through the mainly Chinese enclave of Jelutong and they beat him up badly, thinking he was a Malay. He wasn't, he was a Gurkha, and he finally made his way back to camp.

When his comrades found out what had happened, there was a call for retribution and the battalion was turned out. In full fighting order they marched through Jelutong and the 'tiddley winks' (chinks), so brave when beating one man, had no stomach for taking on his mates and they ran! We knew the chinks couldn't fight unless they heavily outnumbered their opposition. Forget Bruce Lee; he was one in twenty million.

The next day, patrols were out, Gurkha, police, both civil and military and us. Our tactical HQ was the main police station on Penang Road and from there we went on patrol with the Military Police, all thoughts of bombs forgotten. Before boarding the Land Rover, we found that we wouldn't be armed but would carry the ubiquitous pick handle.

The British military authorities must have had a lot of confidence in their soldiers and considered them supermen if they thought that hordes of rioters would run at the sight of sappers with pick helves. Only once in the east did I ever carry a rifle in a civilian setting and that was in Singapore, when the Malaysian race riots of 13th May 1969 spilled over to the Republic, and we formed armed riot squads.

So, we 'tooled up' in different ways. Dave Woolmer carried a Gurkha kukri; most carried machetes and I had an SMG bayonet. I'd cut off most of the large locking ring, which immediately identified it as WD property. It had been given to me by an armoury storeman of 2 RGJ. The OC took one look at us and exclaimed that there was a lot of fearsome weaponry on display that day and so there was, but he never told us to leave it behind and we felt better carrying something other than a piece of wood.

Our opponents, should there be any, were almost certain to be Chinese, as they were and still are, the dominant race on Penang. Our base was the main police station on Penang

Road and from there we went out, patrolling the mainly British families' areas, always with at least two Land Rovers. We drove through a town that showed plentiful evidence of rioting and violence. People had been murdered on the streets, premises and vehicles burnt and all for a few cents difference in the exchange rate.

The Malaysian Army was drafted in from Kuala Lumpur, complete with armoured cars. We saw a mosque in Glugor turn-out, irate Malays shouting and gesticulating, heading for the small area where the Brits and Chinese lived but an armoured car came down the road and stopped them. They wouldn't disperse until the commander of the vehicle pointed the machine gun at them and we saw them bolt, sarongs held up and hightailing it back into the mosque. The trouble lasted for nineteen days, days of twenty-four hour curfews, patrols and violence that eventually claimed twenty seven lives, with one hundred and thirty injured and one thousand three hundred arrested.

Some of the fatalities were from curfew breaking but most were the result of racial friction, Malay against Chinese with the Indians, being a minority, caught in the middle but still suffering. Few in Malaysia today know anything about this riot. We know because it made an impact on our lives. The memories of those days have lived with me. It was out of the question for me to see Karen and we continued our romance by letter.

Chapter Fourteen

The RAF launch was withdrawn until the New Year, leaving us with no escort vessel so dumping was postponed, and we went back to Sungai Nibong to do more locating. The Prolines were not in working order, so we had to use hand augers and we put down several holes.

The bomb locator then picked up readings of items resembling large metal drums and the consensus of opinion was that they held torpedo warheads. Some forty-gallon drums of oil were also found. In another tunnel was found five strange objects that turned out to be mine clearing devices, each of which contained 30 pounds of HE.

A shaft was started in the middle of one of the longest tunnels. It was estimated that whatever was there was a long way down, about thirty-five feet. Plant took about fifteen feet of soil from the surface, and it was also used to start the shaft, which was eight feet by thirteen and a half. The backacter was used to get within striking distance of the tunnel's contents. At about eighteen feet, sea mines were uncovered. Using plant to do the preliminary work was a brainwave. The joys of working in a confined space below the surface in the prevailing temperature, with very high humidity, were nil and we were thankful that we had to spend little time there.

We had no knowledge of Japanese mines so this was a job for the Navy. The Fleet Clearance Team at Singapore was contacted and an officer and CPO came up. A mine was lifted out of the shaft by the Bray, a mine in very good condition. It still had readable labels on it, should any of us have been capable of reading them. After being inspected by the Naval EOD members, the mine was emptied, the explosive burnt and the primer was blown up. The Navy confirmed that the large metal boxes did contain torpedo warheads.

Another tunnel was worked on, and many shells were found, along with a set of railway lines. Locals had been in there at some stage and the cartridge cases from the shells had been chopped off, presumably with an axe. Other shells were found and identified as German 105mm (4 inch) anti-aircraft ordnance. Further along, net mines were discovered and some 250kg bombs. These were all left in situ as Christmas was upon us.

My birthday falls on December 23rd and that year it was on a Saturday and a gang of us converged on the town to celebrate in our usual way. First stop was the Tiger Bar on Chulia Street and from there we gravitated to the Pathe Bar, which was our normal hang-out. A lot of beer was consumed, and this was the last time that Les Wardle came out with us. I know he was there because I have a photo of him and the back of it is dated. Why he was there I don't know, unless it was to help me celebrate because his wife had arrived from the UK, and he'd settled in a quarter out at Jalan Gajah. We visited him on a few occasions and drank his beer with him, but things had obviously changed and we seldom saw him outside of working hours. I can remember sitting in the front compound of his home, helping him to remove cattle ticks from the ears of a mongrel he'd adopted. His wife was welcoming (not all army wives are!) and I found that she came from Warnham, the Sussex village where I went to school.

Christmas came, my first in a hot country and it didn't feel like Christmas at all. As far as I know, only Tim and Mick had any experience of Christmas in the tropics. Four of us were invited by George and Lou Duncan to spend Christmas Day with them. Others had been invited by Les Wardle, John Green and Sandy. It is British Army tradition that on this one morning of the year, the OR's are woken by the sergeants and other senior ranks and hot tea laced with whisky or rum is served.

After a night on the beer in the NAAFI, this was a mixed blessing, but I managed to drink it. Later in the day we all went to our various destinations, suitably well dressed and relatively sober and I had a super meal.

Our hosts couldn't do enough for us and after lunch, we spent the afternoon playing marbles on the front porch with the kids. During the evening, John and Wendy Green, who lived nearby, came over and brought their guests with them, including an Aussie, his wife, child and mother-in-law. They were friendly and sociable. There was good-natured rivalry between the 'Poms' and the Aussie and when Bob the Aussie mentioned fitness and his body weight, John Green asked him 'was that with or without?' Bob inquired 'with or without what?' and John replied, 'the ball and chain'. At this there was a lot of shouting about 'Whingeing Poms' and 'Aussie Convicts' but it was all in good fun.

On Boxing Day there was a football match between the garrison members and their wives. The blokes were handicapped by being in pairs and having a leg tied to his neighbour. Most men came in fancy dress, many were just getting over last night's drink and to cap it all, Les Wardle had connected up a fire hose and was liberally spraying everyone in range. There wasn't much resemblance to football, but they all seemed to have a good time.

When we returned to the site after the holiday, we found that the locals had again been digging on their own account and had removed and emptied two torpedo warheads of about 225kg of picric filling, but they also spilled a lot of the explosive. It was a bad place to work, with that stuff left on the ground.

On the next dumping day, we had a different escort, a Royal Malaysian Navy patrol boat; the RAF could no longer supply their craft. Whereas we sometimes returned on the RAF launch, there was no chance of us hitching a lift on the gunboat, so we had a three or four hour trip back to look forward to. The load this trip consisted of 250kg bombs, which Jim Stow and I had to manhandle. It goes without saying that we never lifted them, that was done by the derrick but we had to get them ready on the Uniflote deck ready for hoisting aboard the LCT.

Many a hand had been cut and many fingernails broken and torn doing this job. The bombs were ragged, rough and pitted and the tail fins were sharp.

Using the bomb's lifting lug was out of the question because the metal was rusty and unsafe, but I didn't like our method of hoisting the bombs back then and time hasn't increased my enthusiasm. It just needed one rope to snag or worse, to snap or the bomb to slide over the point of balance and we could be in deep trouble but only for an instant! We were surrounded by sailboats and there must have been plenty of sailmakers around at that time and a word in the right ear and a few dollars could have procured us a reasonable heavy duty, made-to-measure canvas sling. It would have been far safer than a piece of rope. But we were only sappers, and it wouldn't have been prudent to mention this, as SNCO's and officers are paid to know better!

Sgt Duncan guiding a bomb

Stow & Farrow readying a bomb before hoisting onto the LCT
'Lofty Mullen' of the LCT crew hovers in the background

JIM STOW

Jimmy was a decent lad, only about twenty years of age. He'd joined the unit from boy service, where he'd done well. The story was, he'd been a bit of a boxer while in Junior Leaders Regiment but as he never got into any fights, we couldn't judge how able he was. He was good company in a drinking session, and I can't ever recall him being at the staggering stage, so he was able to exercise control. He was always ready to join in a good singsong or on a night out. He spoke with a slight Suffolk burr, what we Londoners called a 'swede' accent. He worked hard and seldom moaned. A good, clean-cut young bloke.

I tracked him down and spoke to him in the early 90's and suggested a meet but he wasn't interested in renewing old friendships, which was a pity.

Jim Stow, Minden Barracks
May 1968

It was mentioned that we had something of a morale problem by knowing the reputation of the job and the dangers involved. Not true! We knew the dangers of bombs back in England, but we were all volunteers and we never worried overmuch about such things back there and this was merely an extension of the overall bomb disposal sphere of operations. If there were any worries, they had to emanate from our leaders, not us.

We were very happy-go-lucky but not overtly so. We had sunshine, plenty of beer, girls. What did we have to worry about? There was no complacency among the troops, who knew full well what could happen if something went badly wrong. The lower ranks in this job certainly didn't let familiarity breed contempt.

On reaching the dumping grounds, the bombs were rolled toward the slide overhanging the sea and then gravity took over. The larger bombs took up so much space that few could be dumped at any one time but it was satisfying to see these relics consigned to their watery grave, where, unless there was an earthquake or similar occurrence, they'd rest forever. I doubt anyone had given any thought to the effects of picric acid leaching into the sea over a number of years and its effect on marine life but if the Malaysian government weren't worried about the ocean around their shores, why should we? Ours not to reason why!

In January 1968 we had two major problems. First we lost two of the team, Bernie Roome and Taff Philips, to chronic hepatitis, brought on by contact with picric acid. Tim Vismer also went down with this but recovered. Unfortunately, both Bernie and Taff were more seriously affected and were 'medevacced', medically evacuated back to the UK. I was sorry to see them go. It meant that our team was starting to lose cohesion. Who was going to be next, I wondered. Tim spent some time in hospital in Butterworth, over on the mainland before rejoining the team.

TAFF PHILIPS

Taff was a completely closed book. Like Scouse Gore, he kept to himself. Despite sitting next to him on the plane on the way out and the subsequent eleven months working with him, I knew nothing about him whatsoever, not even his first name! Where he went and who with, we never knew. He'd dress up in what we called Planters kit, a white shirt, white shorts, white socks and polished shoes and off he'd go. It wasn't a woman he was seeing that we were fairly sure of, so it can only be that he'd got friendly with a family. Wherever he went, he certainly never discussed it. When we drank in the NAAFI, Taff would be conspicuous by his absence. Likewise, if we went out on the town, no Taff! I have many photos of the team relaxing, but Taff isn't in any of them, apart from one single one at Christmas.

He was a hard worker while we were on site but he was in a different section to me, so we never went to sea together. I met him once more in England when I was posted back but after saying hello, we never met up again. I have a suspicion that his health suffered too badly from exposure to picric acid, and he possibly left HM Forces. I was around in Longmoor for months and our paths never crossed again after that first meeting.

**Taff still in Planters mode,
George Duncan's pad**
Christmas 1967.

BERNIE ROOM

Unlike Taff, Bernie Roome did mix with us. He did drink although not much. A quiet lad, he was never in the forefront of any action or discussion. The on-site photos I have of 'Sailor' generally show him sitting down, watching. He was saving his money to get married and rationed himself. He was generally in-funds but wasn't good for a 'touch'. Rabidly pro-Welsh, I can only assume he was Welsh by descent. Taff Philips spoke Welsh, spoke English with a Welsh accent and had a Welsh name. Sailor, however had no obvious connection to Wales but he was certainly Welsh by inclination and was always comparing England to his chosen country, with England coming out second best. I can remember his last birthday celebration in the NAAFI. Unusually, he ended up paralytic and had trouble standing up. He did manage it eventually and he lifted his glass and toasted Wales, with Cymru am Byth, and he then brought up all the beer he'd drunk, covering his shirt and shorts in vomit before collapsing like a pole-axed ox. He was cleaned up and put on his bed. Bernie, like Gordon Whipp, died in 2016.

Sailor Roome, Broadbridge Heath
1966

Japanese bombs from the World War Two period were very crudely made and very little was known, apart from the very obvious, about the explosive filling of picric acid and its hazards. It was known to be dangerous, as we'd found out with three team members being incapacitated. If inhaled or absorbed through the skin, it could affect the liver and kidneys and in extreme cases result in death but there were no records of its toxicity level. Picric was also used in the torpedo warheads we found.

The middle of January saw the arrival of an Army PR team, intent on taking photos and interviewing us. One photo that ended up in Soldier Magazine had us all laughing. It was of the OC, holding up a bomb locator, while we sat around in a semi-circle. The caption to this was that he was explaining the workings of the detector to the members of the team. We'd had to explain them to him! And where did the PR team get the idea for their main heading 'EVEN EIGHT SUICIDE PLANES!' Someone had been pulling their leg! A photo of Mick Rose adorned the front of the Sapper, the Corps magazine, one member had his interview shown on his local TV station and the rest of us had to be content with having the write-up and photo in their local papers. Mine was included in the North London paper, The Hornsey Journal, which made my old dad very chuffed when he was shown it at the time, although for some strange reason when he got older, he said it was a fake and taken in England.

A fake and taken in England, it most certainly was not! My OG's were black with the sweat of working in the scrub all morning and you don't sweat like that in the UK! I still have the original photo and the newspaper cutting that was kept for me by my sister-in-law.

The Royal Navy EOD team came up from Singapore to help us clear the torpedo warheads and the net mines. They also wanted to retrieve another sea mine from the shaft, which they did. The warheads were removed without difficulty from one site at Sungai Nibong but the net mines from another site at that location were under rock.

The extraction of the mines from this site had to be done by digging from the tunnel entrance. An assortment of munitions were found; ninety six 60kg bombs, incendiary bombs, a bomb weighing 63kg and sixteen net mines. The bombs were dumped without trouble, along with all other smaller munitions recovered but the net mines presented a major problem. Being mines they float, and we couldn't get into the buoyancy chamber, so a decision was made to burn the contents.

The base plates were removed and the contents, type 88 explosive, was taken out. Type 88 was dark grey in colour, a powder made up of silicon carbide, ammonium perchlorate, wood pulp and oil. It's sensitive to friction and has a low point of ignition and burns very fiercely, as we were to find out.

In one bay, we filled plastic buckets with explosive from an opened mine, in the next bay, Sgt Duncan and Les Wardle tipped the powder out in a 'u' shape. One end was then ignited, and the powder burnt. As the powder train burnt, the wind picked up glowing embers and blew them over from the burning site to the next bay, where we were up to our elbows in enough powder to obliterate us. Hot on the heels of the embers came Lance corporal Green who chivvied us away from the mines and out of harm's way and over to the Land Rover before disaster struck. We were lucky but disaster was about to strike elsewhere.

After one powder train had been set off, the buckets of explosive were again tipped out in the 'u' shape, but not enough time had been allowed to elapse between burns and as the explosive hit the ground, it was immediately ignited by embers and both Wardle and Duncan were engulfed in flames. The first thing I knew about this was when Les came staggering toward us, his arms held out at right-angles from his body. We rushed over to him to try to help and with a groan he told us 'don't f****** touch me!' The skin was hanging from his arms like curtain pelmets and most of his flesh was burned and raw. His clothes had gone, apart from his underpants and they, being soaked in sweat, had saved the middle of his body. His hair had melted, and he was in a terrible state.

The ride back to Minden Barracks, with the RAMC escort, over rough ground, in a bucking Land Rover, must have been agony for him and George. We weren't to see Les back at work again, despite the official statement that both men recovered in three months and returned to work. George Duncan came back but Les was at death's door for months. He was sent back to England and eventually discharged from the army due to his injuries. It was only because Les was a tough nut that he pulled through.

When it became apparent that Les wasn't going to rejoin us, we decided to visit his wife and ask if there was any way we could help but on thinking about it, her reputation was going to suffer if eight or nine single men roared up to her house when Les was in hospital, so the brakes were put on that idea. Officialdom took over instead and the Wardle affairs were put in order and Les' wife vacated the house and went back to England. I found later that she also vacated their married life because while he was in hospital, she left him.

The opinion of those of us near the action on that day was that little planning had been done, no thought had gone into the scheme, and someone was in too much of a hurry to get the job completed and without naming names, we all knew who was at fault. I went to the court of inquiry and told them what I saw that day.

Whether my presence at the inquiry made any difference to the outcome is more than I can say but nothing seemed to change so perhaps I wasted my time. This incident cast a blight on our work for a couple of weeks but whatever we felt, it was as nothing compared to what Wardle suffered. The medical cover provided on site, one staff sergeant from the RAMC, complete with small medical pack, was totally inadequate and couldn't begin to cope with an injury like this. We were told some months later that Les was so bad, he probably wouldn't survive. But he did!

A postscript to this; in 1975, while in 16 Field Squadron BAOR and three weeks before my discharge from the army, Les Wardle was posted in. He'd re-enlisted and been posted to Osnabruck. I met him in the Sgt Major's office and shook his hand. His face was pitted and had a grey tinge, testimony to that tragic day in 1968.

He said hello to me and with his lop-sided grin on his face, asked me how I was. I said hello back and told him I was OK and that I was bloody glad to see him. I told him we'd been informed he wouldn't make it, but I was happy to see it wasn't true and that we'd have a get together and have some beers when he got himself sorted out.

I'd already informed the Sgt Major, WO2 Dunn, that Les and I were old friends, just as soon as I heard he was due in, so the man couldn't accuse me, one of his NCO's, of getting too friendly with the troops but I could see that he didn't like it. After what Les Wardle and I had seen and done together, nothing was going to stop me from saying hello to him. Les and I never enjoyed a beer, he was sent straight out on a troop project, and I was gone before he got back, and I never heard of him again.

This was the second case that I knew of extreme burns suffered in Bomb Disposal. A sergeant on ammunition clearance on a Devon beach had been badly burned by an exploding phosphor mortar bomb. It blew him backwards but emptied its burning contents over him. He was picked up and dumped in the sea, then rolled in wet blankets and taken to hospital. He had burns on his face, chest, stomach, hands, and legs and after extensive skin grafts his fingers were webbed.

Ten mines had been left stockpiled, waiting for a decision from the Navy on how to dispose of them and work commenced on digging out the torpedo warheads. A total of thirty-five were found. The cases were thin, and the warhead bodies were made of light gauge metal and with water coming through the ground, the cases had rusted. The picric contents of the warheads had exuded, leaked out and formed a large pool. While removing the warheads, picric acid was dripping from them. Not the best environment to be working in. Each warhead weighed over four hundred pounds, but they were dumped through the bow doors of the LCT without any noticeable problem.

While we were beavering away in the sun, we received news from our parent unit in Kent about the operations our colleagues were involved in, back in England.

One was at St Mary's Hospital, Newport, Isle of Wight. Our old friend Lance corporal Dave Stone was sent there to investigate reports of projectiles being found in two water storage tanks. Dave had to clamber into the tanks and in filthy water, retrieve forty-six projectiles that turned out to be practice smoke mortar bombs. Many had disintegrated or were in the process of.

Another job was in the grounds of Albany Prison, Isle of Wight, where a number of old hand grenades were found; dangerous grenades. Twenty five years had not improved their condition. The prison was built on the site of a former army barracks and if there were a few grenades, there were possibly many more. It took weeks to investigate the grounds. (I saw a 'Mudlarking' programme on You Tube recently where an old 36 Mills Grenade had been found. It was detonated with spectacular results, proving that these weapons are still deadly half a century after being armed.)

Corporals Ken Summers and Dave Stone led a team of twelve Ukrainians who worked at Yapton, Sussex. A scout doing 'bob a job' found a practice bomb and the local kids used it as a plaything. This particular bomb was filled with magnesium and was used for target practice. The area where it was found was known as 'The Jungle' and as the name implies, it was very overgrown. The scrub was removed, and mine lanes were laid using white tapes. 4C mine detectors were used to check the ground for metal objects.

The job was made difficult by the presence of metal rubbish that had accumulated over the years but each warning from the 4C had to be investigated. It was forecast at this time that there was at least twenty years of work for the unit, and it must have been good news for 49 Bomb Disposal Squadron. Although the majority of work would involve the clearance of battle training areas, bombs still did turn up.

One that surfaced was in a quarry at Aldridge. This was a 1000kg bomb, found twenty-six feet down the quarry face and it was found to have an extension cap over the fuse and it couldn't be identified. The cap was taken off with a trepanner, identified and made safe. Corporal Dave Kinnon was on this job, along with Corporal Haines. I'd last worked with Dave on the Lutterworth job and I'd been press-ganged into playing football against him and suffered from it. He was a big man but fast!

Twelve 250kg bombs were found at Larkhill, Salisbury Plain and another murder-weapon hunt was undertaken by the unit. A single 50kg bomb was also recovered in Sussex by Captain Nichols and Lance corporal Pearce. Our parent unit reckoned they had about three hundred bombs on their books, bombs that had been investigated but nothing more. In some cases, the landowners didn't want them removed. Some were on mudflats, well away from the general public and others in even more remote places. A lot of people who knew they lived in close proximity to unexploded aerial bombs ignored them.

One farmer had a VI in one of his fields and only reported it twenty-odd years later when he decided he wanted to plough that particular field. During 1967, a Hampshire farmer had been killed while ploughing. He unearthed and picked up a live two-inch mortar bomb, possibly one of the most dangerous and unstable projectiles. This was found on land that hadn't been used by the army, but the Home Guard had used it for a practice range. Another farmer, in Lincolnshire, was badly injured when he dug up a German anti-personnel bomb that had been dropped near an RAF base. And in 1967 alone, eleven bombs and eight and a half thousand missiles, including mortar bombs had been disposed of. From 1959 to 1967, two hundred bombs had been made safe.

In April we heard that the team had been invited to a garden party given by the Governor of Penang and the invitation was accepted. I'd have been happier with something more tangible than drinking warm pop on someone's lawn. And then came the bombshell, suits will be worn! Suits! It's fine to make that statement but I didn't have one. I went out there with one, but the trousers had gone the way that all trousers go, when the arse came out of them.

Luckily for me, we had with us one Lance corporal Shepherd, who was our personal RAOC rep. Now I knew that he had a suit, but could I get it off him for the day? I started buying him beer and cups of tea. He said I was a crawling sod and asked me what the hell I wanted. I explained about the invite and my predicament and would he consider lending me his suit for just one afternoon. At first, he flatly refused but I asked him did he want me to let down the entire unit by going in scruff order. And then he brought up the fact that I always referred to his corps as the 'Rag and Oil Company'. I told him it was all in jest.

He agreed to lend me his suit but then said he hoped I'd pay for any damage to it, and I wasn't to be sick down the front of it. They must have had some fine parties in the RAOC! I told him that our hosts were all Muslims and that there was no booze and at worse, he might get lemonade down the front of his 'whistle'.

We went to this 'do'. I'd picked up a natty little grey straw trilby from somewhere, which I must admit made me look a bit like a gangster's apprentice and which brought forth some sardonic comments from the others but what the hell it was only for a few hours! Margaret, the wife of Joe Hawkins, one of our plant ops, held my arm as we made our grand entrance. I'd never been to a function like this before and neither had anyone else in the team. We were as out of place as a navvy at No.10. John Green, Bob Nesbitt and I went looking round this place but it was more being nosy than anything else. We wandered into a kitchen and other rooms at the back of the house. There wasn't much to see. Someone made a speech, but it was lost on me and I can remember very little of that afternoon.

We were all happy when it was over and we could make our way back to camp, get out of restricting clothes and into flip-flops and shorts again. Shep's suit didn't suffer and I bought him beers.

**Farrow before the
Governor's Garden Party**
April 1968

Some idiot at, or near the top, brought in a rule that we had to dress properly while in our own NAAFI. Shorts and flip-flops would do while we lay about in our rooms but not in our bar. There, we had to wear long trousers and shoes. Asked why, we were told that the wives of married team members would object at the sight of testicles hanging below the bottom of the shorts.

We countered this with the fact that we didn't wander into the homes of the married personnel uninvited, and they shouldn't just walk into what was our living room. Our argument fell on deaf ears, and we were over-ruled. We never knew who instigated this, whether it was a pad's wife or one of our interfering seniors, but it led to reduced bar takings when some of us refused to use the bar and there was a definite cooling off in the attitude to pads from then on.

I already had my free time booked and not going into the bar was no hardship to me. I only used it once after that. There was a cook shop in camp which generally catered for the locals, but I used it sometimes when I wanted food, even though it was out of bounds to us. They made good fried rice, and it was cheap and I'm sure the boss thought that my money was as good as the next man's.

It was coming up to the time when we'd be posted to Singapore and I for one was in no hurry to go. I was completely settled where I was, I had a five-day working week, good food and a knowledge of my immediate future. Added to this was the fact that I was in no rush to leave my girlfriend. There was no guarantee that we'd see each other again after I was posted south. And then we were told that we'd all been given the opportunity of spending time with the FCDT in Singapore and learning some of their tasks. We'd entertained them and they'd seen how we operated and now they were reciprocating.

Opportunity? I didn't look at it like that and I had other ideas. I was none too happy, and I applied to see the OC with a view to being excused. I had my interview, and I was asked why I didn't want to go and explained but it made no difference and I'd be going with the rest. Authority was never overjoyed at the prospect of a British soldier getting entangled with a local girl so maybe they thought that if we were separated, I'd lose interest.

Separation was the normal ploy but it doesn't always work, as I'll explain later.

We went to Singapore on the train, and it was slow! At one stage, Bob Nesbitt and I got off and walked along the track and we made better progress than the train. It's 482 miles from Penang to Singapore and the train stopped at every little station. It was an all-day job. When we got to Singapore in the evening we were collected and taken to the shore base, HMS Terror and allocated beds with the FCDT. One bed is much like another, and we soon settled in. We stayed in the mess that night, far too tired to venture out to the bright lights or even the NAAFI. I was billeted next to a stocky Able Seaman diver named Bernie. He had a German surname, but I won't identify him. He had the largest collection of porn literature, if indeed you can call it literature, that I've ever seen.

These yellow editions were known by servicemen throughout the east as Hong Kong Bibles. Presumably that's where they were printed but I wouldn't know. He was very protective of his library, keeping it under lock and key and never lending it out.

Our first day there, and all others, we spent with the clearance divers, watching and learning. Being no good in the water myself, I thought their job far more difficult than ours. I couldn't imagine having to work under water, where visibility and movement is limited. Having tried the diver's face mask, I found it very restrictive, and those oxygen tanks weighed a ton!

I didn't know at that time that underwater, the tanks weighed much less. Or they should have done but I had a big surprise coming. Our first time in the harbour started from the jetty, about fifteen feet above water level. To the old hands this was fine, but I'd never jumped into the sea before. The tanks we used were of the double variety. I had these strapped on and was told to jump but on no account let the mouthpiece come out.

There was a red-haired petty officer diver in charge, called 'Ginger' (who else?) and he was dispatching us. He told me to jump. OK, I jumped and the shock of hitting the water and then being submerged almost made me lose the mouthpiece. I had to control myself and take steady breaths. I went down like a brick and hit bottom! I'd been told to fin upwards when I was in the water but try as hard as I could, I couldn't move. My feet were buried in the mud of Singapore Harbour and there they stayed. I had ample time to look around and notice the old bike frames, tin cans and assorted rubbish that probably always finds its way into harbours, but which is only visible at close range.

The water was cloudy and far too murky to see any distance. The next thing I knew was Greeny jumping in, grabbing me under the arms and pushing me to the surface. He was free-swimming so must have been a good swimmer. When I got out of the water, Gordon and Greeny were having hysterics.

The tanks we'd used had flat lead plates inserted between them in a special compartment and these two had loaded mine to capacity. No wonder I couldn't move down there. I called them a pair of bastards and really meant it. It was bad enough going in. Not being able to move, was, in 'squaddy' language, kicking the arse out of it! I didn't see the funny side of this and told Greeny that I wasn't going in again. I did, but only when the two of them apologised.

Had I known then what I know now, nothing would have got me to enter the water again; no inducement, no threats, no B252's, nothing! Sometime previously, a Naval diver had been killed by a shark in the self-same harbour and he would have been an experienced diver, not a first-time novice like me. Had there been a prowling carnivore around at the time I went in, with me not being able to move, I would have been a dead man! Before going in the water again, I made sure that the lead plates were adjusted to my weight.

Green and Whipp in the tank room, no doubt 'fixing' mine

I learned to move around down there, and we did some underwater acetylene work, cutting up scrap metal, which isn't easy under twenty feet of water. The flame continually went out due to being at the incorrect distance from the object being cut. I still wasn't good at being submerged but it got easier as time went on. I suppose it's a case of getting used to it. We weren't there long enough for me to do that, but I did finally enjoy what I was doing. As it turned out, I wasn't the only one who felt uneasy about working underwater.

One of the delights of being in Terror was the daily rum issue. When we arrived, we were all asked if we were old enough to drink, did we drink or were we teetotal. I don't recall anyone admitting to being T. A green card was issued to each of us stating our name, rank, which mess we lived in, religion, the lot and if we were G, T or UA, Grog, teetotal or under-age. On the back of my card is a stamp which has, at the top, an indecipherable series of letters, taken from the MOD Lexicon and HMS TERROR at the bottom.

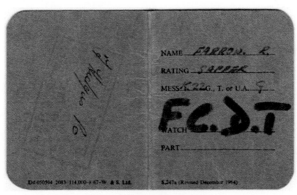

My grog card
No idea why I kept it but glad I did

It has an upside-down signature from a long retired Petty Officer but nowhere is there a date stamp (a slip up by Navy security?) so from what happened prior and immediately after, the nearest I can pin down this visit to Terror is the first half of June.

At the grog issue we had a choice of 'neaters' or half and half. Half a pint of neat rum or rum mixed with water. Imagine half a pint of neat rum in that heat. I settled for half and half and even that was enough. We got used to it though.

After taking that first issue we went happily to the guardroom to leave the base and get a cab to town, and we were stopped! The duty PO said everyone leaving the base had to be smartly dressed and no one was allowed out wearing jeans and that included visiting pongo's. So, we had to go back to the mess to change. A couple of them then decided it was too much trouble and stayed behind while the rest of us went into Singapore for a look around and some beer. That was on a Wednesday afternoon, on 'make and mend', the Navy's answer to recce afternoon. We found our way to a bar where we'd drunk sixteen months before, a bar run by a taciturn, see everything, miss nothing Mr. Lee.

It was a white-tiled place in Chinatown and while getting up to go to the toilet, I knocked a glass over. Lee commented that I'd done the same on my last visit. Bloody hell, I thought, he's got a good memory. We had a few beers there, bade goodbye to Mr. Lee and wandered off to other bars. That was the only time we went drinking in town. HMS Terror was in the north of the island while Singapore town was right at the southern end, a considerable journey and hardly worthwhile, considering most of us would be posted to units in that area soon. It could wait.

The trip back up north was a repetition of the trip that took us down. After a late start on a dull and overcast morning, we had a slow, clanking, stop-start routine that jolted us back and forth and gave birth to some very caustic comments on the professionalism of the employees of the Peninsular Railway.

We'd been told to stay on the train and so we didn't get out and walk alongside the track this time. We could have done so safely while in Singapore, but the communist threat was still ongoing in Malaysia and would continue until 1989. Although Chin Peng was up north across the Thai border, thousands of his supporters and many of his henchmen weren't. On the way down, without knowing it, Bob and I had taken a bit of a chance.

BOB NESBITT

Bob was an irrepressible Northern Irishman from Belfast. It was seldom that anyone saw him without his big grin. He was generally a quiet chap, with a sardonic sense of humour. He was great friends with John Green, as they'd worked together on more than one job, and they could rely on each other. Bob was a great one for the ladies and had all the charm of the Irish at his disposal. In a garrison that had few young women, he'd found one. He could hold his drink with the best and if all his countrymen had been like him, there would have been no 'Troubles'.

He never pushed himself forward but was always there when work was to be done. In 1975, while waiting for a flight at Gutersloh, I met Jim Gore, and he told me that Bob had died as the result of an accident. He's remembered with great affection. I owe him my life!

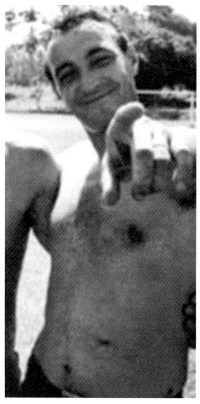

Bob Nesbitt
the smiling Irishman

The arrival of the new team, including a new OC, Major Hoskins and another Jock sergeant, Sgt McDonald spelt the beginning of the end for us although it made no difference to our normal procedure at work. Although we were three men short from the original team, the drivers and plant ops had pitched in when they could and helped with the digging and manhandling. Until the new boys were acclimatised and found their way around, they might as well not have been there.

We carried on digging up 250kg bombs, these being our priority now. The CO Bomb Disposal also made his second appearance on the site and this coincided with the new team's arrival.

We were doing our usual task of removing the bombs when the whole circus descended on us and there were bodies everywhere; getting in the way, asking questions and generally making life difficult. Half a dozen of them clambered down into the pit and tried to help in removing the bombs and we watched Mick Scott trying, on his own, to swing 500 pounds of bomb round on a rope. We had a laugh and decided that, with the CO and the two OC's looking on, he was after a second stripe. He'd arrived as a lance jack, as had Phil Monks.

They'd obviously been promoted just prior to being sent out. They were in the way, there was little they could do, and they were told to step aside. The more at the workface, the more likelihood of accidents. They'd get their chance.

Apart from Scott and Monks, we knew none of these people and they showed us how we must have looked fifteen months before; white skinned and uncertain, with pristine uniforms. We, by comparison must have seemed like scarecrows to them, suntanned, hard-bitten and scruffy. Few of us had matching shirts and shorts.

I even had epaulettes and flashes missing from my shirt. On site we wore what suited us best, jungle boots, DMS boots and in my case, hob-nailed boots. Shirts were only obligatory to travel in, not to work in.

Some wore shorts and some wore longs, some wore berets and some jungle hats or no head wear at all. You can't be smart while digging holes in mud and moving around heavy, rusty hardware and while that day was an exception, there was generally no one else around to see us. I have it on record that ministers, and high-ranking officers and officials came on a weekly basis to view our progress but if they did, we either took no notice or seldom saw them.

We were told later that the CO was impressed with our work. What he thought of our appearance wasn't vouchsafed but as we had no moans from on high, we must assume he wasn't bothered too much.

This batch of 250kg bombs were removed and ferried down to Glugor, then taken out to the LCT. It was to be our final trip out to the dumping ground, and I wanted it to last. The bombs were dispatched using the wooden chute and there were no problems. We had good weather and as always, I used the return journey to sit on deck and enjoy what was to be my last trip on the Ardennes. Knowing beyond doubt that this was the final one, I sat and looked at the phosphorescence thrown up by the LCT screw and watched boats' lights. I knew I wouldn't be seeing this again so wanted to make the most of it.

The Royal Engineers of the Territorial Army also had a Bomb Disposal section and they paid us a visit a week before we were due out. I can remember none of the names or faces of the sappers and only one person sticks in my memory and that was the section corporal. I can see his face now, but his name has long been forgotten. They assisted us on the sites, getting their hands dirty and picking up tips on what to do and what not. It was all good practice, although they would never meet a Japanese bomb again in their lives. It was a big holiday really but why not. We'd also enjoyed something of the same.

It wasn't all hard work and we had had the experience of a lifetime. On our last Saturday night on Penang, four days before our team was posted out, a dance was given for us at the army school. A lot of people were invited, most of whom we didn't know. There were friends and friends of friends and hangers on, all eager for a good time, some music, dancing, and beer. I'd arranged for Karen to accompany me and one of the team and his wife had agreed that she could stay with them after the dance was over. We all had a good time, much beer was drunk and plenty of cuddling on the dance floor. Karen got up and sang 'The Wedding' to me, which I thought was grand. She looked like a dream that night, in a gold satin, tight-fitting sarong kebaya and I could see many of the lads eyeing her up, all to no avail.

The members of the new team were there, but keeping a fairly low profile because this was our night! We'd been presented with a wall plaque before this, an Operations Bomb Penang plaque with the unit bomb depicted. At the commencement of the dance, an MC announced that the dance was in honour of all the work we'd done, there was applause and congratulations and along with the plaque, that was all we were going to get from this job.

We made the best of it though and drank as much beer as we possibly could. I had many dances with my girlfriend. I was never much of a dancer, and she had me beat, hands down but we enjoyed ourselves.

Towards the end of the function, it became apparent that there was serious friction between the couple who were going to put Karen up for the night. The husband became threatening, and Karen told me she was frightened and didn't want to risk going there in case he turned violent. He had done many times before.

So, with this in mind, and although it was past midnight, I decided we'd have to try to get a cab and I'd take her to a hotel in town. That was when George Duncan stepped in and offered to put Karen up at his place if she didn't mind sharing with their toddler, Abigail. Karen agreed and they took her in their transport.

I told them I'd collect her next morning, which I did. She'd been given breakfast and told me she'd had a decent night. I thanked George and Lou for helping out and we went to the ferry. It was fortunate that she never stayed with our warring couple as the husband did hit his wife and might have turned on Karen also. He was a known wife-beater and I blame myself for putting my girl in the position where she may have come to harm.

A member of the new team had unconsciously followed the lead given by our lad who'd thrown himself so wholeheartedly into the local life. From being a quiet, non-drinking, unobtrusive bloke, he changed. He'd been in the habit of sending his money back home to his girlfriend in anticipation of his wedding, but she'd repaid this loyalty by spending it all and calling off the romance. He went completely off the rails at this news, as well he might. All his money was now spent on having the good time he'd deprived himself of. One day he went to Sgt McDonald and asked for an interview with the OC. This was granted and he requested permission to get married to a local girl.

One of the necessities involved when a marriage application went in was for the military police to visit the girl involved. They had to check for any illegal activities or communist leanings in her and her family, who they also visited. (A visit was paid to my prospective bride and her parents, but they found nothing to alarm them.) What they found in this case though was that the future wife wasn't an ordinary girl at all. For one thing, she was about fifteen years older than the applicant. She also had three kids and not to put too fine a point on it, she was on the game.

For obvious reasons this liaison wasn't a good idea, and the unlucky soldier was told to pack his kit and he was posted immediately to Singapore under escort.

Separation! I said it didn't always work and this demonstrates it. At the first opportunity, the man involved came back to Penang and somehow got married in a civil ceremony, thereby by-passing military rules. How the authorities handled it after that I have no idea as the original team were just being posted out, but it showed that separation wasn't always the answer. In this case, refusal had merely stiffened his resolve and made him more determined than ever. I don't know what happened to them; whether they made it work or not but from seeing many similar instances, I'd say it was unlikely.

The trouble with so many 'tarts' who married soldiers, is that when they went to the UK or USA or wherever their husbands came from, they tended to carry on where they'd left off. They earned extra money when their husbands were away and eventually went back home with a bag full of cash, a big photo album of people and places they'd seen and local celebrity status, as those who'd travelled and been around. The authorities did have a headache with this.

Eventually the day dawned that I'd been dreading, the day when we had to leave. Maybe I just wasn't adventurous enough. I was sorry to go, and I think most of them felt the same. We got our kit packed and said our farewells. The TA lads had settled in and they were to temporarily make up the numbers of those of us who were leaving that day.

Being the sentimentalist that I am, I had a good look round at the area we were leaving behind; our bashas, the two little houses at the very perimeter of the camp, where two Malay soldiers from 402 Troop lived with their families and the slope down across the field that cut off half a mile of the trek to the cookhouse.

The Gurkhas used this area for their in-camp training and on many a Saturday morning, we sat outside the basha and watched them creeping toward us. Although the weeds were only about one foot in height, those men could completely disappear into it. And it was by the open drain at the bottom of this slope we'd one day been confronted by a huge cobra. He raised his body, hood spread, and we stopped in our tracks. He was ten feet long, if he was an inch. There was a tentative move backwards; nothing fast enough to alarm the beast and we took the long way round.

We were leaving all this behind. We'd spent over a year in this location and looked on it as home. 'Home is where you hang your hat' is a true saying and could equally well apply in Singapore but what was waiting for us there? Once again, from a small, isolated unit, we were going to a much larger one, with all the ramifications that held. We'd already spent a little time at Gillman Barracks, so we weren't going to somewhere totally unknown, but the barracks were only where we lived, not worked. 59 Squadron was based at Cloutman Lines and 54 Squadron at Morris Lines, both on Ayer Rajah Road.

Tim Vismer, Scouse Gore and I were destined for 54, Mick Rose, Jim Stow, Gordon Whipp and Park for 59 and John Green and Bob Nesbitt went to 11 Squadron at Terendak. Even those of us in Gillman Barracks weren't going to see much of each other. The two squadrons were usually away, seldom crossing paths and so the only chance of us meeting up again was in the cookhouse or NAAFI.

An expert had predicted in the past that the task couldn't be completed without an accident happening and he was right! Two men had died in the late 50's and in the latest attempt, two had suffered horrific burns and two had been medically evacuated. The remainder of us were very lucky to still be in one piece. But we had changed! We weren't the same boys who'd arrived on the island all those months ago.

We'd done a good and worthwhile job, we'd seen life. We'd help rid the island of some very nasty munitions, ranging from aerial bombs to torpedo warheads and a whole range of smaller stuff also.

Our total for the nine months spent on actual disposal, despite breakdowns, hold-ups of necessary equipment, bad weather and lack of dumping vessels, was a very impressive one hundred and fifty tons. Not a bad result and one we could be proud of but the only 'down' factor of this task was the fact that we, who'd proved the job, born the brunt of the locating and hard work, with injuries and accidents thrown in, were posted out almost as if we were in disgrace and that along with the two BEM's awarded, some members of the new team were given Queen's Commmendations for Brave Conduct. Awards were flying about like confetti! If this sounds like sour grapes, yes, I suppose it is but I think the original team deserved better.

We finally threw our suitcases onto the 3-tonner that was to take us to Butterworth, and we set off. The trip to the docks didn't take long and we boarded the ferry. I can remember looking back at the hills of Penang, out over sunlit water that had rainbow coloured oil on the surface. The island looked beautiful from my vantage point on the ferry. We'd seen it at its best. It had to change, it was inevitable, but it changed beyond recognition.

Penang roads were packed with shipping. Shipping I'd steered the Uniflote through one day when I was given the chance of being the 'driver'. I knew that what I'd experienced was something unique and that from that day forward, my life was never going to be the same again.

Personnel

Attached Personnel – RE

Sgt Sanderson

LCpl Piper
Driver

LCpl Edwards
Plant Fitter

LCpl Maxwell
Plant Op.

Spr Flavell
Plant Op.

Spr Floyd
Plant Op.

Spr Johnson
Plant Op

Spr Blalock
Draughtsman

LCpl Grey
Ord Cpl

LCpl Morling
Plant Op

Spr Hawkins
Plant Op

Spr Tobin
Plant Op.

Attached Personnel – Other Arms

LCpl Woolmer RCT
Driver

LCpl Land RCT
Driver

Cpls Manning & Owen RCT
Uniflote

Driver Wells RCT
Driver

Drivers Graham and McCandless RCT
Uniflote

Driver Barclay RCT
Driver

Cpl Derbyshire RCT
Uniflote

Driver Brassen RCT
Driver

Driver Ridley RCT
Driver

LCpl Shepherd RAOC
Storeman

Cpl Clarke RCT
Uniflote

LCpl Warren RAOC
Storeman

French 2RGJ
Driver

Epilogue

Well, all that happened fifty-six years ago and I'm now seventy-eight. Times change and today few would consider swapping their comfortable life for one of removing old and still lethal hardware, but someone has to do it and there's still a lot of it spread around the world. My comrades and I shared some wonderful times and some very bad ones but that was the secret, sharing! I did a further seven and a half years in the army, but I was spoilt by my first thirty months. After that experience, everything seemed to pall by comparison. The other squadrons I went to did the normal sapper jobs of bridge building, water supply, minefield breaching and construction etc., very necessary but to me, lacking in interest. Had I been posted back to Bomb Disposal, I'd probably have stayed in the army.

I married my Karen, whose real name was Lai Yin. I heard and ignored all the advice from the 'mixed marriages never work' brigade, all married to British girls and half of whose own marriages hit the rocks. I applied to get married from the OC of the squadron I was with in Singapore. At twenty-three, we had to ask permission. It beggars belief! Permission granted, I rented a private house. I went to the GPO in town one Saturday morning, drew out all the money from my POSB account and got a cab to the causeway between Singapore and Malaysia. I walked over the causeway and told a cab driver I wanted to go to Malacca, where Karen had landed a job, so she could be nearer to me.

The driver told me it would cost one hundred and fifty dollars but cheaper if he picked up others on the way. I knew I was being robbed but I told him to pick up no one else and to get there quickly. He asked me if I had the fare and I showed him the money. Off we went and it took about three hours. I had the address and the driver found it. I told him to wait for me and I walked in on my girlfriend who was surprised to say the least. I told her we were getting married and to get her things together. She said she wanted to see her boss to collect her wages. He was OK about the short notice and paid up and off we went, back to Singapore.

I took her to a hotel for the night, promising I'd be back the next day. I collected her from the hotel and took her to the house, which was at Sembawang Hills. The house was well equipped with all the necessary kit, three-piece suite, tables and chairs, beds and kitchen kit and she settled in. We were married a month later in a civil ceremony and I moved in with her.

The army priest refused to marry us in church when he found that Karen had been educated by Catholic nuns and I said something about Christian charity. He told me not to be impertinent and I then told him what to do with his church. He then stormed out after telling me he was going to report me to the OC. Tough!

The Church of England has always been short on tolerance. Read Kipling's 'Kim' and the discussion between the RC padre and the Anglican Vicar on the subject of Kim's Lama. The vicar held that the Lama was bound for hell as he was ignorant, primitive and wasn't a Christian while the Church of Rome was much more enlightened and understanding. While I have little time for the Catholic religion as any other, I did find that many RC padres were approachable, unlike their Protestant counterparts.

We were married at Singapore Registry office, and we've been together for fifty-four years, proving that not all marriages have to be held in church and not all mixed marriages fall by the wayside.

One team member was not invited to the wedding and of the seven invited, one was on duty, and one was too drunk from the night before. I was happy that five came and it was the last time I saw some of them.

Living in Asia as I do, there's little chance of meeting any of my old comrades again but I have met a few of them since leaving the forces, Ingrey, Stone, Duncan, Gore and most recently, Green. I'm in contact with others I haven't seen since the old days, courtesy of the internet but by the law of averages, apart from those named in the dedication, many more must have taken that path which we all have to tread one day. To them all, thank you for helping to make it the experience of a lifetime.

Glossary

ACC	Army Catering Corps
Attap Basha	House with bamboo walls and roof
BAOR	British Army of the Rhine
Bull	Cleaning and polishing (most unnecessary)
Char (Hindi)	Tea
Chinese Parliament	Informal discussion
CO	Commanding Officer
Dhobi	Washing clothes
FARELF	Far East Land Forces
FCDT	Fleet Clearance Diving Team (RN Bomb Disposal)
Geordie	Anyone originating from the Durham area.
HE	High Explosive
IED	Improvised explosive device
Jackspeak	Royal Navy parlance
JRC	Junior Ranks Club (NAAFI)
JSBDS	Joint Services Bomb Disposal School

Knocking Shop	Brothel
LSL	Landing Ship Logistics
Mankiest	Dirtiest
MCTC	Military Corrective Training Centre (Military Prison)
MRS	Medical Reception Station
OC	Officer Commanding
oppo	Mate, Friend
OR1	Other Rank Class 1
Pads	Married Personnel
Pongo's	Royal Navy term for Army personnel
POSB	Post Office Savings Bank
PWD	Public Works Department
RA	Royal Artillery
RAOC	Royal Army Ordnance Corps
Rag and Oil Company	As in RAOC (above)
MP's	Royal Military Police
R&R	Rest and Recuperation
RSM	Regimental Sergeant Major (WO1)
Scouse	Any Liverpudlian
Shovel GS	Shovel, general Service
Shovel RE	Shovel, Round Edged

SMG	Sub Machine Gun
SLR	Self-Loading Rifle
SSM	Squadron Sergeant Major (WO2)
SNCO	Senior Non-Commissioned Officer
Stroppy	Quarrelsome / Unfriendly
TA	Territorial Army
TABT	Typhoid, Para-typhoid A&B and tetanus
Taff	Any Welshman
Whistle	Cockney Rhyming Slang – Whistle and flute = suit
WO	Warrant Officer
WOSB	War Office Selection Board
WRAC	Women's Royal Army Corps
WW2	World War 2